SEED AND HARVEST IN A CONCURRENT ERA

KENNETH WALLEY

CIBUNET
Publishing

Published By:
Cibunet Publishing
Email: admin@cibunet.com
Website: www.cibunet.com

TABLE OF CONTENTS

INTRODUCTION

Across the world today, Christians are praying for revival and so an awakening is imminent. We need healing from the leprosy, the scents, blindness, dumbness, deafness, doubt, and guilt that estranges us from God's glory.

The purpose of this book is to bring insights from the scriptures that reflect the present times. It is the result of personal experience as a servant of God with a deep passion to see the goodness of God manifested in the lives of those who love Him. This book does not seek to introduce anything new but to highlight existing truths that we have shied away from in this generation. The ways by which we fall short of God's goodness is primarily when we become ignorant of how His blessings come to us or fail to operate in these virtues. Overall, as the scripture clearly points out, 'there is nothing new under the sun'. Whatever has happened in the past is what tends to repeat itself again.

The evidence of a difficult period in which we live today, requires no prophecy to understand that there is a lot wrong with our generation. In this book, you will learn how spiritual time unfolds in relation to our calling in Christ and the world system. You will gain insights on how the primary objects of worship in the tabernacle enhances our spiritual senses to excel in a higher dimension.

Part I

Seed And Harvest In A Concurrent Era

CHAPTER ONE

THE TIMELESS ERA

The pre-flood period, which is the timeless era, starts out at the onset of creation with Adam and Eve as the only human characters present on earth. The story of creation outlined in the book of Genesis chapter one and two reveal the process of God's works that show patterns of how He functions throughout the scriptures. God initially declares His intentions and then manifests them systematically with time. Most of the things He declared in Genesis chapter one existed spiritually after calling them out. While some of creation manifested immediately, some were like promises waiting to manifest. In Chapter two we see how He makes man through a physical process of molding earth. He plants a garden and makes animals that are named by Adam. Essentially the entire work of creation involves both instantaneous and systematic processes.

Adam and Eve, the first couple violated the rules of their residence in the Garden of Eden and were evicted. They had been deceived by Satan who influenced them to act against God's instructions. God passed judgment not only on Adam and Eve, but also on the serpent who was Satan's instrument in the Garden of Eden: "So the LORD God said to the serpent: "Because you have done this, You are cursed more than all cattle, And more than every beast of the field; On your belly you shall go, And you shall eat dust all the days of your life. And I will put enmity between you and the woman, and between your seed and her Seed; He shall bruise your head, And you shall bruise His heel" Genesis 3:14, 15. The interesting and most significant aspect of the curse on the deceiver is when God says 'And I will put enmity between you and the woman, between your seed and her seed; He shall bruise your head, and you shall bruise his heel'. God's antidote to the deceiver was going to be 'SEED'. The seed of the woman will conquer the deceiver! The potential to overcome the deceiver is embedded in the seed. Seed is reference to the offspring of the woman. It is fundamental to understand that every human being is a seed sent from God with the potential to crush the schemes of the devil.

Seed And Harvest In A Concurrent Era

Adam and Eve were now outside the original place God had intended to prosper them because of their sin, so we can say they were in 'enemy territory'. "Now Adam knew Eve his wife, and she conceived and bore Cain, and said, "I have acquired a man from the LORD." Then she bore again, this time his brother Abel. Now Abel was a keeper of sheep, but Cain was a tiller of the ground. And in the process of time it came to pass that Cain brought an offering of the fruit of the ground to the LORD. Abel also brought of the firstborn of his flock and of their fat. And the LORD respected Abel and his offering, but He did not respect Cain and his offering. And Cain was very angry, and his countenance fell. So the LORD said to Cain, "Why are you angry? And why has your countenance fallen? If you do well, will you not be accepted? And if you do not do well, sin lies at the door. And its desire is for you, but you should rule over it." Now Cain talked with Abel his brother; and it came to pass, when they were in the field, that Cain rose up against Abel his brother and killed him. Then the LORD said to Cain, "Where is Abel your brother?" He said, "I do not know. Am I my brother's keeper?" And He said, "What have you done? The voice of your brother's blood cries out to Me from the ground. So now you are cursed from the earth, which has opened its mouth to receive your brother's blood from your hand. When you till the ground, it shall no longer yield its strength to you. A fugitive and a vagabond you shall be on the earth." And Cain said to the LORD, "My punishment is greater than I can bear! Surely

Seed And Harvest In A Concurrent Era

You have driven me out this day from the face of the ground; I shall be hidden from Your face; I shall be a fugitive and a vagabond on the earth, and it will happen that anyone who finds me will kill me." And the LORD said to him, "Therefore, whoever kills Cain, vengeance shall be taken on him sevenfold." And the LORD set a mark on Cain, lest anyone finding him should kill him" Genesis 4:1-15.

Outside the Garden of Eden, Adam and Eve conceived and gave birth to Cain and Abel. Seed was now birthed on earth, so God saw an opportunity to manifest His judgment on the deceiver. He inspired Cain and Abel to offer up sacrifices to Him. God hoped that through the sacrifice He would be able to usher in the blessing of 'Time', to demarcate and establish a limit on the works of the devil. As a result of the curse unleashed on Adam and Eve, there was a totally chaotic environment here on earth. "To the woman He said: "I will greatly multiply your sorrow and your conception; In pain you shall bring forth children; Your desire shall be for your husband, And he shall rule over you." Then to Adam He said, "Because you have heeded the voice of your wife, and have eaten from the tree of which I commanded you, saying, 'You shall not eat of it': "Cursed is the ground for your sake; in toil you shall eat of it all the days of your life. Both thorns and thistles it shall bring forth for you, and you shall eat the herb of the field. In the sweat of your face you shall eat bread till you return to the ground, for out of it you were taken; for dust you are, And to dust you shall return" Genesis 3:16-19. A curse gives demons a mandate to execute judgment against man. It is obvious that Adam, Eve and their two sons Cain and Abel were victims of demonic activity, emotional and financial hardships. However, the curse on the deceiver was God's plan to ameliorate man's plight. This is the reason that God inspired a sacrifice from Cain and Abel. He was giving them an opportunity to enter a covenant relationship that will empower them to have dominion over the works of the devil. God gave them the standards for this sacrifice – firstling, flock, and fat. Abel's sacrifice met these standards, so God accepted it. Cain however did not meet the standards set so his sacrifice was rejected. He became sad and developed a negative attitude, but God encouraged him and suggested that he should do the right thing. Cain will not yield to divine counsel and rather murdered Abel. As the first born of Adam and Eve, Cain had blown up the opportunity to usher in the blessing of 'time'. He was cursed, so demons now had the liberty to run the affairs on earth. In those days, the demons were visibly obvious and so Cain pleaded with God to preserve him from their punishment.

The lifestyle and story about the descendants of Cain give a clue as to the state of the earth in the timeless era. "Then Lamech said to his wives: "Adah and Zillah, hear my voice; wives of Lamech, listen to my speech! For I have killed a man for wounding me, even a young man for hurting me. If Cain shall be avenged sevenfold, then Lamech seventy-sevenfold" Genesis 4:23&24. Lamech, who was the fifth descendant of Cain was the first known polygamist. He murdered two people who had offended him. Social disorder and crime had become the norm. "Now it came to pass, when men began to multiply on the face of the earth, and daughters were born to them, that the sons of God saw the daughters of men, that they were beautiful; and they took wives for themselves of all whom they chose. And the LORD said, "My Spirit shall not strive with man forever, for he is indeed flesh; yet his days shall be one hundred and twenty years." There were giants on the earth in those days, and also afterward, when the sons of God came in to the daughters of men and they bore children to them. Those were the mighty men who were of old, men of renown. Then the LORD saw that the wickedness of man was great in the earth, and that every intent of the thoughts of his heart was only evil continually. And the LORD was sorry that He had made man on the earth, and He was grieved in His heart. So the LORD said, "I will destroy man whom I have created from the face of the earth, both man and beast, creeping thing and birds of the air, for I am sorry that I have made them" Genesis 6:1-7. To compound the problem on earth, the demons that were visible at the time began to have sexual relations with humans. Their offspring were a crossbreed of demons and humans. These were wicked gigantic beings who perpetuated all kinds of evil on earth. It was so bad that God regretted creating man and resolved to end the timeless era by destroying man.

When Adam and Eve realized that Cain had murdered Abel, destroying the chance for a time era, they conceived again. "And Adam knew his wife again, and she bore a son and named him Seth, "For God has appointed another seed for me instead of Abel, whom Cain killed." And as for Seth, to him also a son was born; and he named him Enosh. Then men began to call on the name of the LORD" Genesis 4:25&26. Notice that they named Seth as Abel's replacement. The reason is that though Abel's sacrifice was accepted by God, the consequent blessing of 'a time era' could not manifest because he was murdered. Since he had no offspring, there was no beneficiary for the blessings of Abel. Worst of all, Cain was the firstborn and because he was now cursed, there was no chance for God's blessings to manifest here on earth unless there was another seed with the potential to substitute Abel. Seth was named as a replacement of Abel and raised to believe in the essence of sacrifice. It was the generation of Seth that sought to get it right by walking with God. "And as for Seth, to him also a son was born; and he named him Enosh. Then men began to call on the name of the LORD." The descendants of Seth developed a relationship with God even though they were living in a timeless era and were victims to all the evil of that period. We can compare them with genuine Christians living in today's world of corporate greed and rampant wickedness in society.

"Seth lived one hundred and five years, and begot Enosh. After he begot Enosh, Seth lived eight hundred and seven years, and had sons and daughters. So all the days of Seth were nine hundred and twelve years; and he died. Enosh lived ninety years, and begot Cainan. After he begot Cainan, Enosh lived eight hundred and fifteen years, and had sons and daughters. So all the days of Enosh were nine hundred and five years; and he died. Cainan lived seventy years, and begot Mahalalel. After he begot Mahalalel, Cainan lived eight hundred and forty years, and had sons and daughters. So all the days of Cainan were nine hundred and ten years; and he died. Mahalalel lived sixty-five years, and begot Jared. After he begot Jared, Mahalalel lived eight hundred and thirty years, and had sons and daughters. So all the days of Mahalalel were eight hundred and ninety-five years; and he died. Jared lived one hundred and sixty-two years, and begot Enoch. After he begot Enoch, Jared lived eight hundred years, and had sons and daughters. So all the days of Jared were nine hundred and sixty-two years; and he died. Enoch lived sixty-five years, and begot Methuselah. After he begot Methuselah, Enoch walked with God three hundred years, and had sons and daughters. So all the days of Enoch were three hundred and sixty-five years. And Enoch walked with God; and he was not, for God took him. Methuselah lived one hundred and eighty-seven years, and begot Lamech. After he begot Lamech, Methuselah lived seven hundred and eighty-two years, and had sons and daughters. So all the days of Methuselah were nine hundred and sixty-nine years; and he died. Lamech lived one hundred and eighty-two years, and had a son. And he called his name Noah, saying, "This one will comfort us concerning our work and the toil of our hands, because of the ground which the LORD has cursed." After he begot Noah, Lamech lived five hundred and ninety-five years, and had sons and daughters. So all the days of Lamech were seven hundred and seventy-seven years; and he died. And Noah was five hundred years old, and Noah begot Shem, Ham, and Japheth" Genesis 5:6-32. The godly descendants of Seth reveal how the stage was set for the flood that destroyed the evil people from the earth as an end of the timeless era.

Enoch, one of the descendants of Seth is said to have walked with God, and so God took him away from this earth. Enoch named his son 'Methuselah' who became the longest man that ever lived. The reason Methuselah lived so long was because of the prophetic mandate by which he was named. Because the descendants of Seth worshipped God, they invoked the favor of God for the promise of a 'time era'. Consistent with the character of God, this promise was reinforced from one generation to another. Enoch is described as a prophet in that era and named his son Methuselah which means two things, 'javelin' and 'when he is gone it shall be sent'. Methuselah was to become the bomb that destroys the timeless era. His prophetic destiny was to orchestrate the end of the cursed period where demons run the show on the earth. Methuselah will not die until the stage was set for an end of the timeless era so the time era could begin. God kept promising the descendants of Seth that he will send rain on to the earth as a blessing for their sacrifices. During the timeless era, rain had not yet been introduced to the earth. "This is the history of the heavens and the earth when they were created, in the day that the Lord God made the earth and the heavens, before any plant of the field was in the earth and before any herb of the field had grown. For the Lord God had not caused it to rain on the earth, and there was no man to till the ground; but a mist went up from the earth and watered the whole face of the ground" Genesis 2:4-6. Temporarily, a mist watered the earth to sustain vegetation. There were no clearly defined seasons and no demarcation of time as we have it today. During the timeless era, things happened haphazardly. There were no time patterns and planning was virtually impossible. Characteristics of the timeless era included not being able to predict a harvest or the end of a period of adversity. Sacrifice was the key to unfold the blessing of 'time' but then Cain had missed the opportunity to invoke its manifestation on earth. The descendants of Seth sacrificed offerings to God, so they became heirs of the promise of 'time'. God promised to send rain to the earth so all the descendants of Seth were in anticipation of the flood that will end the timeless era. Lamech, who was the son of Methuselah had a son and named him 'Noah', a prophetic mandate meaning, 'This one will comfort us concerning our work and the toil of our hands, because of the ground which the LORD has cursed'. Clearly, the evidence of the Adamic curse was in full force during the timeless era. Reinforced by the curse on Cain, demons had a field day and the prevalence of evil and struggle was unimaginable.

The Flood

Lamech named his son Noah as a prophetic mandate to end the timeless era – "This one will comfort us concerning our work and the toil of our hands, because of the ground which the LORD has cursed." Noah was given the assignment to build the ark because of this mandate. "This is the genealogy of Noah. Noah was a just man, perfect in his generations. Noah walked with God. And Noah begot three sons: Shem, Ham and Japheth. The earth also was corrupt before God, and the earth was filled with violence. So God looked upon the earth, and indeed it was corrupt; for all flesh had corrupted their way on the earth. And God said to Noah, "The end of all flesh has come before Me, for the earth is filled with violence through them; and behold, I will destroy them with the earth. Make yourself an ark of gopher wood; make rooms in the ark, and cover it inside and outside with pitch. And this is how you shall make it: The length of the ark shall be three hundred cubits,

its width fifty cubits, and its height thirty cubits. You shall make a window for the ark, and you shall finish it to a cubit from above; and set the door of the ark in its side. You shall make it with lower, second, and third decks. And behold, I Myself am bringing floodwaters on the earth, to destroy from under heaven all flesh in which is the breath of life; everything that is on the earth shall die. But I will establish My covenant with you; and you shall go into the ark—you, your sons, your wife, and your sons' wives with you. And of every living thing of all flesh you shall bring two of every sort into the ark, to keep them alive with you; they shall be male and female. Of the birds after their kind, of animals after their kind, and of every creeping thing of the earth after its kind, two of every kind will come to you to keep them alive. And you shall take for yourself of all food that is eaten, and you shall gather it to yourself; and it shall be food for you and for them." Thus Noah did; according to all that God commanded him, so he did" Genesis 6:9-22. The flood God had promised the descendants of Seth was now imminent. Methuselah could not die until the stage was set for the judgment of man. Those who were guilty of not acknowledging God with acceptable sacrifices will be destroyed while those who were righteous had to be preserved. Noah was given the divine assignment of constructing an ark to preserve the righteous through the flood. The most important standard for an acceptable sacrifice is the firstling, which is fulfilling one's divine assignment. God gave Noah specifications for the construction of the ark. Before now, there had never been an ark or even a boat. The whole earth was one massive land mass. It was after the flood that the earth was split into the various continents as it is today. Noah had to work closely with God to build this ark that will preserve the righteous. Noah was instructed to bring seven each of all the clean animals and birds as well as two each of unclean animals to preserve alive in the ark.

Methuselah died in the year Noah completed the ark. It was time for judgment that the world was not expecting and so they probably mocked Noah for building the ark. To compound their ignorance, rain from heaven or even a flood had never manifested before, so it was all strange talk in their ears. It was business as usual while they continued in their evil ways and practiced wickedness until Noah entered the ark with his family and all the animals as prescribed by God. Then God closed the ark and sent the flood for forty days and forty nights. All the people of the timeless era who were not in the ark were destroyed.

Poverty and wickedness are a bad mix for any human society, and today we see evidence of both in our world. In the years ramping up to 2012, I observed traits of the timeless era in the lives of many good Christians. Harvest, tranquility and prosperity were generally unpredictable so I sought God prayerfully for insight and He referred me to a prophecy of scripture in the book of Daniel chapter seven:

Seed And Harvest In A Concurrent Era

"In the first year of Belshazzar king of Babylon, Daniel had a dream and visions of his head while on his bed. Then he wrote down the dream, telling the main facts. Daniel spoke, saying, "I saw in my vision by night, and behold, the four winds of heaven were stirring up the Great Sea. And four great beasts came up from the sea, each different from the other. The first was like a lion, and had eagle's wings. I watched till its wings were plucked off; and it was lifted up from the earth and made to stand on two feet like a man, and a man's heart was given to it. "And suddenly another beast, a second, like a bear. It was raised up on one side, and had three ribs in its mouth between its teeth. And they said thus to it: 'Arise, devour much flesh!' "After this I looked, and there was another, like a leopard, which had on its back four wings of a bird. The beast also had four heads, and dominion was given to it. "After this I saw in the night visions, and behold, a fourth beast, dreadful and terrible, exceedingly strong. It had huge iron teeth; it was devouring, breaking in pieces, and trampling the residue with its feet. It was different from all the beasts that were before it, and it had ten horns. I was considering the horns, and there was another horn, a little one, coming up among them, before whom three of the first horns were plucked out by the roots. And there, in this horn, were eyes like the eyes of a man, and a mouth speaking pompous words. "I watched till thrones were put in place, And the Ancient of Days was seated; His garment was white as snow, And the hair of His head was like pure wool. His throne was a fiery flame, Its wheels a burning fire; A fiery stream issued and came forth from before Him. A thousand thousands ministered to Him; Ten thousand times ten thousand stood before Him. The court was seated, And the books were opened. "I watched then because of the sound of the pompous words which the horn was speaking; I watched till the beast was slain, and its body destroyed and given to the burning flame. As for the rest of the beasts, they had their dominion taken away, yet their lives were prolonged for a season and a time. "I was watching in the night visions, And behold, One like the Son of Man, Coming with the clouds of heaven! He came to the Ancient of Days, And they brought Him near before Him. Then to Him was given dominion and glory and a kingdom, That all peoples, nations, and languages should serve Him. His dominion is an everlasting dominion, Which shall not pass away, And His kingdom the one which shall not be destroyed.

"I, Daniel, was grieved in my spirit within my body, and the visions of my head troubled me. I came near to one of those who stood by, and asked him the truth of all this. So he told me and made known to me the interpretation of these things: 'Those great beasts, which are four, are four kings which arise out of the earth. But the saints of the Most High shall receive the kingdom, and possess the kingdom forever, even forever and ever.'"Then I wished to know the truth about the fourth beast, which was different from all the others, exceedingly dreadful, with its teeth of iron and its nails of bronze, which devoured, broke in pieces, and trampled the residue with its feet; and the ten horns that were on its head, and the other horn which came up, before which three fell, namely, that horn which had eyes and a mouth which spoke pompous words, whose appearance was greater than his fellows. "I was watching; and the same horn was making war against the saints, and prevailing against them, until the Ancient of Days came, and a judgment was made in favor of the saints of the Most High, and the time came for the saints to possess the kingdom. "Thus he said: 'The fourth beast shall be a fourth kingdom on earth, which shall be different from all other kingdoms, And shall devour the whole earth, Trample it and break it in pieces. The ten horns are ten kings who shall arise from this kingdom. And another shall rise after them; He shall be different from the first ones, And shall subdue three kings. He shall speak pompous words against the Most High, Shall persecute the saints of the Most High, And shall intend to change times and law. Then the saints shall be given into his hand for a time and times and half a time. 'But the court shall be seated, And they shall take away his dominion, To consume and destroy it forever. Then the kingdom and dominion, and the greatness of the kingdoms under the whole heaven, Shall be given to the people, the saints of the Most High. His kingdom is an everlasting kingdom, And all dominions shall serve and obey Him.'" This is the end of the account. As for me, Daniel, my thoughts greatly troubled me, and my countenance changed; but I kept the matter in my heart."

The key aspects of this prophecy are:

1. Worldly kingdoms or systems that would be in control of this earth.
2. Believers will encounter a period where the devil will attempt to change time or re-enact the timeless era.
3. Judgment of these worldly systems by the reign of Jesus Christ.

Since our focus in this chapter is on the timeless era, I will explain the second point about believers encountering a period where the devil will attempt to change time. The kingdom of darkness is aware that 2012 is the end of their dominion over the world. Those in the world of occult have indicated that they are unable to predict world events beyond the year 2012, and so they predict erroneously that 2012 may be the end of the world. The truth is that the kingdoms or systems by which the world is controlled will come under judgment, so their fate is no longer clear to them. The years ramping up to 2012 is when we see the devil attempt to change the times on good Christian believers. The devil knows that his time is short and so he has increased demonic activity on the earth to frustrate believers so they may give up on their faith in God. If you have been walking faithfully with Christ in the last decade up until 2012, you will agree with me that though you are faithful in tithing, offerings and the pursuit of purpose; the manifestation of harvest, tranquility and prosperity has generally been a mirage. Whenever something good is about to happen, somehow there is a disruption that snatches it away. The devil has forced the manifestation of a timeless era to weaken the faith of believers and caused some to reject God in their hearts.

CHAPTER TWO

THE TIME ERA

The flood overwhelmed the earth and destroyed all those who were not in Noah's ark. After the flood, Noah came out of the ark and the first thing he did was amazing! "Then Noah built an altar to the LORD, and took of every clean animal and of every clean bird, and offered burnt offerings on the altar. And the LORD smelled a soothing aroma. Then the LORD said in His heart, "I will never again curse the ground for man's sake, although the imagination of man's heart is evil from his youth; nor will I again destroy every living thing as I have done. "While the earth remains, Seedtime and harvest, Cold and heat,

Winter and summer, And day and night Shall not cease" Genesis 8:20-22. Noah offered an acceptable sacrifice that touched the heart of God. This kind of sacrifice was exactly what was required of Cain, but he was unwilling to offer it. God's plan was to give full functionality to the sun, moon, and stars to manifest time. Noah got it right, and God orchestrated the 'blessings of a time era' that will place a limitation on demonic activity on earth. Day and night; seedtime and harvest; cold and heat; winter and summer; represent the four components of the blessing of 'time'.

A. Night or Day

When the sun is up and there is light everywhere, we call it day. Within every twenty-four-hour cycle, we also experience night where the sun sets and there is darkness. The scripture generally refers to believers as children of the day because we are expected to walk in the light of God's word. Most of the activities that God's word tells us not to engage in, do not appeal to the general sense of right, so people often do them under the cover of darkness. For instance, adultery, theft, witchcraft, murder and so on, all take place mostly under the cover of darkness. Day is spiritually synonymous with righteousness, whereas night indicates unrighteousness. "For behold, the day is coming, burning like an oven, and all the proud, yes, all who do wickedly will be stubble. And the day which is coming shall burn them up," Says the LORD of hosts, "That will leave them neither root nor branch. But to you who fear My

Seed And Harvest In A Concurrent Era

name The Sun of Righteousness shall arise with healing in His wings; and you shall go out and grow fat like stall-fed calves. You shall trample the wicked, for they shall be ashes under the soles of your feet on the day that I do this," Says the LORD of hosts" Malachi 4:1-3. The prophet here foretells an era when those who walk in righteousness will surely prevail over the unrighteous. Enterprises and institutions that are built on unrighteous premises will not survive the test of time. In this era, the cycle of days followed by an approximately equal time of night will become unpredictable. Unusually long nights may occur unexpectedly and there will be major disruptions to time as we know it. A typical example is the Covid-19 Pandemic, which is now in its fourth year, and despite our advancements in medical science, this virus is still ravaging our world and slaying so many lives.

However, the impact of righteousness will be clearly visible, as people will see evidence of healing and positive changes wherever the principles of God's word are applied. Your status as either righteous or unrighteous will determine how people will relate to your work. For instance, as a medical doctor who applies divine principles to your work, your patients will experience immediate impact of righteousness because of the healing power of God that will manifest to validate your methods. As a result, you will become the preferred choice of those seeking medical help.

B. Seedtime and Harvest

Agriculturally, farmers cultivate various crops at different times of the year. Though the span of time between sowing and reaping for each crop is different, farmers generally know how long it takes to harvest a crop after it is sown. When you are hired to do a job, you expect to be paid at a specified time. Investors want to know the time frame for expecting dividends. Business loans and interests must be paid up at specific times. The contract for executing a project must be drafted for execution within a time frame.

Predictability is the core of planning which undergirds every form of pursuit. The Capital Markets of the world today operate fundamentally on the element of predictability. Stocks rise and fall based on predictable patterns such as weather, politics, sociological factors, economic indicators, and risk mitigation. Stockbrokers and investors usually follow historical trends to formulate their set patterns of investment. Many have been so successful at this that they have crafted theories and designed investment tools based on their premise of how to invest successfully in stocks, bonds, and mutual funds. The financial brokers with a high rate of success, have attracted a dedicated constituency of clients from whom they constantly raise massive amounts of capital to invest on their behalf.

Prior to the time era, it was impossible to predict harvest, so the investment climate was very bad, and poverty prevailed. For instance, in the timeless era, if a farmer cultivated land and sowed seeds, he could not tell when harvest will manifest. He simply waited it out until the crops matured for harvest. In the time era however, farmers can predict the period for the harvest of any crop they cultivate. So, you see that fundamentally the economies of today's world strongly hinge on the element of predictability facilitated by time, which was a blessing Noah earned by offering an acceptable sacrifice.

"Verily, verily, I say unto you, except a corn of wheat fall into the ground and die, it abides alone: but if it die, it brings forth much fruit." John 12:24. Jesus Christ declared this truth to indicate the sacrifice of his life by which the people of this world could be saved. This salvation is deliverance from all the ways by which the kingdom of darkness holds people captive such as chronic infirmities, emotional frustration, financial frustration and so on. The death of Jesus Christ on the cross was the seed by which deliverance from demonic oppression would manifest as a harvest for those who get saved. Seed is anything that can multiply itself. As humans, we are spirit, we have a soul and live in a body. Throughout the scriptures, the human spirit is referred to as seed. For those who are saved, Jeremiah 2:21 says: "Yet I had planted you a noble vine, a seed of highest quality. How then have you turned before Me into the degenerate plant of an alien vine?" Like a farmer who carefully inspects grains to select highest quality seeds to sow in the field, God chose to save us because of the inherent potentials for a great harvest. "But you are a chosen generation, a royal priesthood, a holy nation, His own special people, that you may proclaim the praises of Him who called you out of darkness into His marvelous light; who once were not a people but are now the people of God, who had not obtained mercy but now have obtained mercy." 1 Peter 2:9,10.

We are a chosen seed, saved by the seed of God's word. "Having been born again, not of corruptible seed but incorruptible, through the word of God which lives and abides forever." 1 Peter 1:23. Our human spirit that is a chosen seed, is adopted by God's word that is an incorruptible seed, through the salvation of our Lord Jesus Christ. God's word is a quickening force that continues to reshape our spiritual nature with an aim for the image and likeness of God to be restored in us. "For the word of God is quicken and powerful, and sharper than any two-edged sword, piercing even to the division of soul and spirit, and of joints and marrow, and is a discerner of the thoughts and intents of the heart." Hebrews 4:12. The impact of God's word on the believer is a continues process through the various feasts that are scheduled for divine encounters. From the Hebrew word 'Moed', they are appointed times when God visits for various forms of quickening of our human spirit:

Seed And Harvest In A Concurrent Era

Sabbath is the divine visitation for our sanctification. Sanctification means cleansing. "...Christ also loved the church and gave himself for it; that he might sanctify and cleanse it with the washing of water by the word, that he might present it to himself a glorious church, not having spot, or wrinkle, or any such thing; but that it should be holy and without blemish." Ephesians 5:25b-27. There are several problems we face that are because of spots, wrinkles, and blemishes in our human spirit. In the same way, that leprosy or skin diseases impact our image, these defamations of the human spirit may result in disfavor and rejection. God's word has a cleansing effect that removes these spots, wrinkles, and blemishes when we are convicted and repent at the word. Many of the healings recorded of Jesus Christ in the scriptures, took place on the Sabbath day. This signifies the essence of constant sanctification of our human spirit. "And let us consider one another in order to stir up love and good works, not forsaking the assembling of ourselves together, as is the manner of some, but exhorting one another, and so much the more as you see the Day approaching." Hebrews 10:24,25. Weekly fellowship that is scheduled for local Church assemblies facilitate the sanctification of the Sabbath. It is essential that we honor this appointed time for sanctification of our human spirit.

Passover is the divine visitation for our consecration. Consecration means to be dedicated to God by sacrifice.

Seed And Harvest In A Concurrent Era

This is the essence of the cross where Jesus Christ offered himself up as a sacrifice. "Purge out therefore the old leaven, that ye may be a new lump, as ye are unleavened. For even Christ our Passover is sacrificed for us" 1 Corinthians 5:7. Though many Christians today take lightly the essence of the Passover, it is an important divine visitation where we are quickened to die to the vices that allow demonic powers to enslave us. The Apostle Paul declared in Galatians 2:20: "I am crucified with Christ: nevertheless, I live; yet not I, but Christ lives in me: and the life which I now live in the flesh I live by the faith of the Son of God, who loved me, and gave himself for me." During the Passover, God's people ate unleavened bread for a week. This was significant of death to the various vices that made us hypocrites. This feast was a commemoration of the redemption of God's people from bondage so, through fasting and prayer for deliverance, victory was established over demonic powers. Passover is the divine encounter where the Holy Spirit reveals the path to overcome inherent vices. Often, this may require us to give up on certain practices that serve as tokens for demonic activity in our lives. Such tokens may include items such as artifacts we own that may be charged by demons, certain food that invoke demonic activity because of ancestral covenants and the avoidance of certain festivities where demonic activity is invoked.

Seed And Harvest In A Concurrent Era

First-fruits is the divine visitation that quickens us with resurrection life. Jesus Christ rose from the dead on the third day by the quickening of the Holy Spirit. "But if the Spirit of him that raised up Jesus from the dead dwell in you, he that raised up Christ from the dead shall also quicken your mortal bodies by his Spirit that dwelleth in you." Romans 8:11. Jesus Christ died on the cross and rose from the dead on the third day. The three days of death might mean three weeks or months or years of death to an inherent vice by the method prescribed by the Holy Spirit. In every area where we die to our vices at Passover, we are also quickened by the resurrection life of Christ during first fruits.

Pentecost is the divine visitation for the fulness of harvest. After his resurrection from the dead, Jesus Christ instructed His disciples to remain in Jerusalem until they were endued with power from on high. "When the Day of Pentecost had fully come, they were all with one accord in one place. And suddenly there came a sound from heaven, as of a rushing mighty wind, and it filled the whole house where they were sitting. Then there appeared to them divided tongues, as of fire, and one sat upon each of them. And they were all filled with the Holy Spirit and began to speak with other tongues, as the Spirit gave them utterance." Acts 2:1-4. Here for the first time, the disciples of Jesus who waited on the instruction of Jesus experienced the outpouring of God's Spirit that empowered them with the spiritual gifts. Three thousand souls were saved on that day and supernatural manifestations of God's power became common among the disciples from that day onward.

Trumpet is the divine visitation for the blessings of divinity. Here, we are quickened to align ourselves with the ministry of angels. Jesus Christ experienced the ministry of angels throughout His life. One instance was after being tempted by the devil, scriptures say: "Then the devil left him, and, behold, angels came and ministered unto him." Matthew 4:11. In the same way that angels ministered to Jesus, we ought to experience the ministry of angels in our lives. "Are they not all ministering spirits, sent forth to minister for them who shall be heirs of salvation?" Hebrews 1:14. Angels are very orderly beings and function as an army. To experience their ministry, we must be orderly and remain in alignment with God's will. The divine visitation of the feast of trumpets aligns our human spirit to foster an increase of angelic activity around us.

Atonement is the divine visitation that establishes peace between us and God. Our sins are atoned for by the Blood of our Lord Jesus Christ. "For in Him dwells all the fullness of the Godhead bodily; and you are complete in Him, who is the head of all principality and power. In Him you were also circumcised with the circumcision made without hands, by putting off the body of the sins of the flesh, by the circumcision of Christ, buried with Him in baptism, in which you also were raised with Him through faith in the working of God, who raised Him from the dead. And you, being dead in your trespasses and the uncircumcision of your flesh, He has made alive together with Him, having forgiven you all trespasses, having wiped out the handwriting of requirements that was against us, which was contrary to us. And He has taken it out of the way, having nailed it to the cross. Having disarmed principalities and powers, He made a public spectacle of them, triumphing over them in it." Colossians 2:9-15. On the Day of Atonement, which is a heavenly courtroom scenario, God's people demonstrate contrition through fasting and prayer. This way, Satan's accusations and sin mandates are terminated by the advocacy of our Lord Jesus Christ. Atonement restores our dominion over the kingdom of darkness.

Tabernacles is the divine visitation that commemorates our destiny. Jesus Christ manifested here on earth to unveil God's glory to mankind. "For whom he did foreknow, he also did predestinate to be conformed to the image of his Son, that he might be the firstborn among many brethren. Moreover, whom he did predestinate, them he also called: and whom he called, them he also justified: and whom he justified, them he also glorified." Romans 8:29-30. The visitation of tabernacles reawakens our quest to dwell on the promises of God and pursue divine destiny. Tabernacles is the point where we reside in the glory of God's presence.

In any arena of life where our human spirit arrives at Tabernacles, a unique presence of God issues out of the blessings of our sanctification, consecration, resurrection, harvest, divinity, dominion, and glory. Anyone who comes under this tent experiences the manifestation of this divine presence.

C. Cold and Heat

To be cold spiritually is significant of 'apostasy', which is the state of rejecting a buoyant relationship with God. The opposite of cold is heat, which is spiritually significant of the state of 'revival'. Most theologians today agree that prophetically, today's Church looks very much like the description given of the Laodicean Church to the Apostle John in Revelation 3:14-22, "And to the angel of the church of the Laodiceans write, 'These things says the Amen, the Faithful and True Witness, the Beginning of the creation of God: "I know your works, that you are neither cold nor hot. I could wish you were cold or hot. So then, because you are lukewarm, and neither cold nor hot, I will vomit you out of My mouth. Because you say, 'I am rich, have become wealthy, and have need of nothing'—and do not know that you are wretched, miserable, poor, blind, and naked— I counsel you to buy from Me gold refined in the fire, that you may be rich; and white garments, that you may be clothed, that the shame of your nakedness may not be revealed; and anoint your eyes with eye salve, that you may see. As many as I love, I rebuke and chasten. Therefore be zealous and repent. Behold, I stand at the door and knock. If anyone hears My voice and opens the door, I will come in to him and dine with him, and he with Me. To him who overcomes I will grant to sit with Me on My throne, as I also overcame and sat down with My Father on His throne. "He who has an ear, let him hear what the Spirit says to the churches." The twenty-first century is notably the only time in history where we can boast of so many mega churches and so many financially rich people claiming Christianity as their religion. Yet there is so much evil in society, it is unbelievable to fathom that Christians exist in society. Approximately half of all Americans claim to be Christians who attend Church, but then the level of moral decadence and corruption is so high. Nominal Christianity is the perfect description of lukewarm Christianity in the time era. People who claim to be Christians only attend Church when it is convenient, obey God at their own discretion and subscribe to a moral standard below what is required by the scriptures. Lukewarmness can be understood by four questions that dot the preflood era: Where are you? Where is your brother? Where is your father? Where is your ark?

Where Are You? The devil manifested through a serpent and deceived Adam and Eve to violate the rules of their space that is, the Garden of Eden. "So when the woman saw that the tree was good for food, that it was pleasant to the eyes, and a tree desirable to make one wise, she took of its fruit and ate. She also gave to her husband with her, and he ate. Then the eyes of both of them were opened, and they knew that they were naked; and they sewed fig leaves together and made themselves coverings. And they heard the sound of the Lord God walking in the garden in the cool of the day, and Adam and his wife hid themselves from the presence of the Lord God among the trees of the garden. Then the Lord God called to Adam and said to him, "Where are you?" So he said, "I heard Your voice in the garden, and I was afraid because I was naked; and I hid myself." And He said, "Who told you that you were naked? Have you eaten from the tree of which I commanded you that you should not eat?" Genesis 3:6-11. Every domain has a king that is clothed with royalty. A naked king is one who violates the rules of their space. Prior to their sin, Adam and Eve were clothed with the glory of God. After they succumbed to the devil's inspiration and sinned, they lost their covering and immediately felt naked and afraid. They made themselves clothes from fig leaves and yet hid themselves from the presence of God. Today, people generally own a lot of clothes, and the rich flaunt their expensive designer wears. However, as was the case of Adam and Eve in the Garden of Eden, Jesus Christ describes the Laodicean Church as 'naked'. Isaiah 64:6 says: "But we are all like an unclean thing, and all our righteousness are like filthy rags; we all fade as a leaf, And our iniquities, like the wind, have taken us away". Jesus counseled the Laodiceans to buy 'white garments' from Him to cover their nakedness. In Christ, we are assigned a domain and if we abide by the divine guidance of truth, we become clothed with the righteousness of God.

Where is your brother? God wanted to change the plight of Cain and Abel who were suffering on account of the sin of their parents – Adam and Eve. He inspired Cain and Abel to offer up a sacrifice and set the standards. While Cain did not meet this standard so his sacrifice was rejected, his brother Abel met the conditions of firstling, flock and fat so his sacrifice was accepted. Cain became very sad and his countenance fell. "So the Lord said to Cain, "Why are you angry? And why has your countenance fallen? If you do well, will you not be accepted? And if you do not do well, sin lies at the door. And its desire is for you, but you should rule over it." Now Cain talked with Abel his brother; and it came to pass, when they were in the field, that Cain rose up against Abel his brother and killed him. Then the Lord said to Cain, "Where is Abel your brother?" He said, "I do not know. Am I my brother's keeper?" And He said, "What have you done? The voice of your brother's blood cries out to Me from the ground. So now you are cursed from the earth, which has opened its mouth to receive your brother's blood from your hand. When you till the ground, it shall no longer yield its strength to you. A fugitive and a vagabond you shall be on the earth." Genesis 4:6-12. When God realized that Cain's attitude was taking him downhill on the slippery slope, God approached Cain and offered him a solution - "if you do well, will you not be accepted?" Cain did not take divine counsel and murdered his brother Abel. God's judgement against Cain was that "A fugitive and a vagabond you shall be on the earth." This sounds like the lukewarm conditions of the Church of Laodicea – "wretched and miserable". Family is the first recorded institution of the scriptures which is the framework for our basic alliances. Interestingly, Cain's sarcastic question – "Am I my brother's keeper?" sheds light on our core responsibility to one another. We cannot harbor unforgiveness, bitterness and malice to remain our brother's keeper. A lukewarm Church is where people walk in pretense. We pretend to love one another but then our actions show contrary.

Where Is Your Father? In Genesis chapter five, there is a record of the descendants of Adam through the lineage of Seth. Among several children born to this lineage Enosh, Cainan, Mahalalel and Jared are mentioned in the scriptures. "Jared lived one hundred and sixty-two years, and begot Enoch. After he begot Enoch, Jared lived eight hundred years, and had sons and daughters. So all the days of Jared were nine hundred and sixty-two years; and he died." Enoch lived sixty-five years, and begot Methuselah. After he begot Methuselah, Enoch walked with God three hundred years, and had sons and daughters. So all the days of Enoch were three hundred and sixty-five years. And Enoch walked with God; and he was not, for God took him". Genesis 5:18-24. Enoch the seventh generation from

Seed And Harvest In A Concurrent Era

Adam disappeared because God took him away from this earth. Assuming someone asked his son Methuselah – "Where is your father?" He would answer – God has taken him away. "Why?" – "He walked with God". Fast-forward several years later, we see another instance - Elijah was caught up into heaven by whirlwind. "And so it was, when they had crossed over, that Elijah said to Elisha, "Ask! What may I do for you, before I am taken away from you?" Elisha said, "Please let a double portion of your spirit be upon me." So he said, "You have asked a hard thing. Nevertheless, if you see me when I am taken from you, it shall be so for you; but if not, it shall not be so." Then it happened, as they continued on and talked, that suddenly a chariot of fire appeared with horses of fire, and separated the two of them; and Elijah went up by a whirlwind into heaven. And Elisha saw it, and he cried out, "My father, my father, the chariot of Israel and its horsemen!" So he saw him no more. And he took hold of his own clothes and tore them into two pieces. He also took up the mantle of Elijah that had fallen from him, and went back and stood by the bank of the Jordan. Then he took the mantle of Elijah that had fallen from him, and struck the water, and said, "Where is the Lord God of Elijah?" And when he also had struck the water, it was divided this way and that; and Elisha crossed over. Now when the sons of the prophets who were from Jericho saw him, they said, "The spirit of Elijah rests on Elisha." And they came to meet him, and bowed to the ground before him. 2 Kings 2:9-15. Elijah is a unique character whose spiritual root is not apparent in the scriptures. He is described in 1 Kings 17:1 – "And Elijah the Tishbite, of the inhabitants of Gilead, said to Ahab, "As the Lord God of Israel lives, before whom I stand, there shall not be dew nor rain these years, except at my word." King Ahab had married the infamous Jezebel and Israel was deeply into Baal and Asherah worship. Elijah who was by then not a famous prophet, suddenly accosts the king with a message - "As the Lord God of Israel lives, before whom I stand, there shall not be dew nor rain these years, except at my word." God had prepared the prophet Elijah in obscurity and yet the words of this man of God took effect over the elements so there was no rain for about three years. King Ahab conscripted a search party to go look for Elijah but could not find him until Elijah showed up again. On mount Carmel, Elijah killed the prophets of idolatry, invoked the fire of God and revival broke out in Israel. Jezebel got offended and threated to kill Elijah. Elijah is tired and seeks to retire so God assigns him to anoint Elisha to take over his ministry. Elisha serves Elijah diligently and sees the point where Elijah transitions into the heavens. "Then it happened, as they continued on and talked, that suddenly a chariot of fire appeared with horses of fire, and separated the two of them; and Elijah went up by a whirlwind into heaven. And Elisha saw it, and he cried out, "My father, my father, the chariot of Israel and its horsemen!" So he saw him no more...." It is important to mention that Elisha was a largescale farmer when Elisha called him into God's service. This status did not interfere with how Elisha submits to the mentorship of Elijah. "My father, my father" is a very humbling way Elisha perceived and served Elijah. From this point onwards, Elisha takes over the ministry of Elijah and became the eyes of Israel. The Christian Church today is experiencing a blindness that fits the description of our Lord Jesus for the Church in Laodicea. It is very confusing when you listen to notable Christian leaders attempting to rein in on political issues and defending their political persuasions as being divine and yet the manifestations are contrary. Christian leaders seeking to be accepted as being 'mainstream' publicly endorse unbelievers who seem to have acquired the so called status of stardom. Many Christians are not rooted in the fundamentals of Christ and would quickly leave a local assembly and join another, when they are rebuked for wrongdoing. The true sense of spiritual fatherhood and sonship is lacking in today's Church, hence a 'blindness' to God's corporate plans for the Church.

Where Is Your Ark? The final straw that 'broke the back of the camel' was the corruption of Noah's day. "This is the genealogy of Noah. Noah was a just man, perfect in his generations. Noah walked with God. And Noah begot three sons: Shem, Ham, and Japheth. The earth also was corrupt before God, and the earth was filled with violence. So God looked upon the earth, and indeed it was corrupt; for all flesh had corrupted their way on the earth. And God said to Noah, "The end of all flesh has come before Me, for the earth is filled with violence through them; and behold, I will destroy them with the earth. Make yourself an ark of gopherwood; make [g]rooms in the ark, and cover it inside and outside with pitch. And this is how you shall make it: The length of the ark shall be three hundred cubits, its width fifty cubits, and its height thirty cubits. You shall make a window for the ark, and you shall finish it to a cubit from above; and set the door of the ark in its side. You shall make it with lower, second, and third decks. And behold, I Myself am bringing floodwaters on the earth, to destroy from under heaven all flesh in which is the breath of life; everything that is on the earth shall die. But I will establish My covenant with you; and you shall go into the ark—you, your sons, your wife, and your sons' wives with you." Genesis 6:9-18. In the face of the deep corruption and evils of that generation, God instructed Noah to build an ark. Like an architect handing over the blueprint of an edifice, God provided Noah with specifications for this ark that would preserve his family from the impending flood waters. Noah built this ark and when the flood came, it wiped out the population of the known world and God started over with Noah and his family.

This is the only period of known history where many Christians can boast of being very rich and yet like the Church in Laodicea, Jesus Christ described their riches as 'corrupted'. Many Christians exploit their employees and engage in business practices contrary to the scriptures. "Come now, you rich, weep and howl for your miseries that are coming upon you! Your riches are corrupted, and your garments are moth-eaten. Your gold and silver are corroded, and their corrosion will be a witness against you and will eat your flesh like fire. You have heaped up treasure in the last days. Indeed the wages of the laborers who mowed your fields, which you kept back by fraud, cry out; and the cries of the reapers have reached the ears of the Lord of Sabaoth. You have lived on the earth in pleasure and luxury; you have fattened your hearts [e]as in a day of slaughter. You have condemned, you have murdered the just; he does not resist you." James 5:1-6. In Revelations 3:18, Jesus said to the Christians in Laodicea, "I counsel you to buy from Me gold refined in the fire, that you may be rich". Whatever is our profession or enterprise, we must have the attitude of Noah and adopt divine truths so that our works would build the ark that preserves us in the face of any evil manifestations.

A revival is about to break forth in the Body of Christ. This revival may not diminish in strength until Christ returns. Unbelievers who reject Christ will turn deeply into the occult in an attempt to survive and shall perpetuate evil publicly. You may encounter such wicked people at work, in positions of authority and generally in society, who will stand as an obstruction to anything good or godly. Believers on the other hand can only survive the wickedness of apostate people if only they are spiritually buoyant in their relationship with God. A revived believer is one who is consistently prayerful and maintains a dynamic covenant relationship with God. Such believers will experience signs, wonders, and miracles in every area of their lives. You must stay on fire with your faith in God to prevail over the workers of iniquity.

D. Winter or Summer

The weather seasons, Autumn, Winter, Spring and Summer show how God visits the earth with manifestations of weather changes to foster a balance of the ecosystem. Prior to the manifestations of the weather seasons, there was a river in the Garden of Eden that served their functions. "And a river went out of Eden to water the garden; and from thence it was parted, and became into four heads. The name of the first is Pison: that is it which compasseth the whole land of Havilah, where there is gold; And the gold of that land is good: there is bdellium and the onyx stone. And the name of the second river is Gihon: the same is it that compasseth the whole land of Ethiopia. And the name of the third river is Hiddekel: that is it which goeth toward the east of Assyria. And the fourth river is Euphrates." Genesis 2:10-14. The river Pison relates to Autumn, Gihon corresponds to Winter, Hiddekel tallies with Spring and Euphrates with Summer. "There is a river, the streams whereof shall make glad the city of God, the holy place of the tabernacles of the most High. God is in the midst of her;

she shall not be moved: God shall help her, and that right early." Psalms 46:4,5. The rivers Pison, Gihon, Hiddekel and Euphrates signify the various ways by which the Holy Spirit equips us in each season to embrace and harmonize ourselves with God's works.

Autumn: This is the first in the weather season cycles and is the time of the former rains. The former rain is significant of God's revelation that shows us how to invest our life, time, and resources. During Autumn, farmers are prompted by the former rains to prepare their soil and sow seeds. There are different kinds of seeds for the various aspects of our human existence. "And out of the ground made the Lord God to grow every tree that is pleasant to the sight, and good for food; the tree of life also in the midst of the garden, and the tree of knowledge of good and evil." Genesis 2:9. The 'tree pleasant to the sight' is significant of the tree of our emotional, marital and destiny. The 'tree good for food' is significant of our financial destiny. The 'tree of life' is significant of our spiritual destiny. The 'tree of the knowledge of good and evil' speaks of the carnal mind. Fundamentally, a tree is cultivated by sowing a seed, so in any area of life where we desire harvests, we ought to sow the relevant seeds.

The relevant seed for any aspect of our life is unveiled by the river Pison. Pison means 'to grow fat'. "And the Lord shall guide thee continually, and satisfy thy soul in drought, and make fat thy bones: and thou shalt be like a watered garden, and like a spring of water, whose waters fail not." Isaiah 58:11. Pison is the river that flows to make fat our bones. It is the flow of divine revelation that requires us to invest our life, time and resources in this arena. Whenever the crust of divine revelation points us toward training, personal-development, volunteering, sacrificing or investing in a specific area, it is evidence of the manifestation of the river Pison. It is an indication that we are in the Autumn season of that area of our existence, and we must endeavor to diligently sow these seeds.

Winter: Winter is significant of a season of adversity and people generally stay indoors away from the cold and snow. Most outdoor recreational activities halt in winter. The green lawns and flowers that decorate the exterior of our homes, landmark facilities, and gardens all disappear and everywhere looks mostly bare and flat. People who are out-doors are often trying to get away from the cold. There is often very little we can do to avoid the winter though it is so predictable.

Snow is what typically manifests in the winter. "For as the heavens are higher than the earth, so are my ways higher than your ways, and my thoughts than your thoughts. For as the rain cometh down, and the snow from heaven, and returns not thither, but waters the earth, and makes it bring forth and bud, that it may give seed to the sower, and bread to the eater: So shall my word be that goes forth out of my mouth: it shall not return unto me void, but it shall accomplish that which I please, and it shall prosper in the thing whereto I sent it." Isaiah 55:9-11. We see clearly here that the snow is part of what makes the earth blossom to facilitate fruitfulness.

During winter, the river Gihon is what flows into our lives to furnish us to overcome the adversities of the season. Gihon means 'to burst forth'. The seeds sown during autumn burst forth out of their shells and germinate. They grow from the soil into another space that is different and austere. These seeds must survive the harshness of winter before they can have the chance to bear fruits. For those of us who live in temperate areas of the world, winter is a season for high gas, electric and heating bills. Winter is meant to get you reflecting on the stewardship of your life. Did you work hard enough in the previous year to accumulate enough to sustain you through winter? Such thoughts and many more flood your mind during the harsh realities of winter. The rational response is that you start to conceive a plan to accomplish more, fight for more, push harder for more. "Therefore being justified by faith, we have peace with God through our Lord Jesus Christ: By whom also we have access by faith into this grace wherein we stand, and rejoice in hope of the glory of God. And not only so, but we glory in tribulations also: knowing that tribulation worketh patience; And patience, experience;

and experience, hope: And hope makes not ashamed; because the love of God is shed abroad in our hearts by the Holy Ghost which is given unto us." Romans 5:1-5. The adversities of winter translate into how God shapes our character to be creative, resilient, and hopeful. Winter is when we reflect on those vices that have kept us limited and constrained. We resolve to confront our negative attitudes, fears, and other inhibitions at all costs. If you spend all winter under the sheets, simply hoping that the season would pass after three months, then you have missed the purpose of the season. Winter never goes away because the physical weather has changed, its adverse impact would continue to repeat itself year after year in your life until you are psychologically transformed and make those plans to 'burst forth'. In any area of life where we experience seemingly unending adversities, it is often because we have not yielded to the convictions of the Gihon River.

Spring: This is the season of the latter rain. The latter rain is God's revelation that shows us how to profit from our investments. "Ask the Lord for rain in the time of the latter rain. The Lord will make flashing clouds; He will give them showers of rain, grass in the field for everyone." Zechariah 10:1. We are told to ask for the latter rain because it signals the end of winter. Spring is the season for trees to shoot forth new leaves and flowers that translate into fruits. People come out of their sheltered mindsets with a deep craving for anything that is outdoors. There is an inherent desire for new space, which is how we make a profit in our endeavors. Interestingly, the river that corresponds to Spring is 'Hiddekel'. It means 'arrow' and signals divine revelation for warfare. Spring is the season when kings go out on military campaigns to either recover lost territory, secure their existing territory, or conquer new territory. Whatever was a king's premonition during the winter determined the kind of military campaign they embarked on during spring.

"In the spring, at the time when kings go off to war, David sent Joab out with the king's men and the whole Israelite army. They destroyed the Ammonites and besieged Rabbah. But David remained in Jerusalem. One evening David got up from his bed and walked around on the roof of the palace. From the roof he saw a woman bathing. The woman was very beautiful, and David sent someone to find out about her. The man said, "She is Bathsheba, the daughter of Eliam and the wife of Uriah the Hittite." Then David sent messengers to get her. She came to him, and he slept with her. (Now she was purifying herself from her monthly uncleanness.) Then she went back home. The woman conceived and sent word to David, saying, "I am pregnant." So David sent this word to Joab: "Send me Uriah the Hittite." And Joab sent him to David. When Uriah came to him, David asked him how Joab was, how the soldiers were and how the war was going. Then David said to Uriah, "Go down to your house and wash your feet." So Uriah left the palace, and a gift from the king was sent after him. But Uriah slept at the entrance to the palace with all his master's servants and did not go down to his house. David was told, "Uriah did not go home." So he asked Uriah, "Haven't you just come from a military campaign? Why didn't you go home?" Uriah said to David, "The ark and Israel and Judah are staying in tents,[a] and my commander Joab and my lord's men are camped in the open country. How could I go to my house to eat and drink and make love to my wife? As surely as you live, I will not do such a thing!" Then David said to him, "Stay here one more day, and tomorrow I will send you back." So Uriah remained in Jerusalem that day and the next. At David's invitation, he ate and drank with him, and David made him drunk. But in the evening Uriah went out to sleep on his mat among his master's servants; he did not go home. In the morning David wrote a letter to Joab and sent it with Uriah. In it he wrote, "Put Uriah out in front where the fighting is fiercest. Then withdraw from him so he will be struck down and die." 2 Samuel 11:1-15.

At the season when kings went out for battle, King David stayed at home. He had become complacent as king and sent Joab the commander of the army with the army to fight for him. What King David did not realize was that the enemy was not only human but demonic. When the demonic forces realized that King David had decided not to come out for war, they came and engaged him in spiritual warfare. He went on top of the roof of the palace and saw a married woman by name Bathsheba taking a shower. He became enticed and committed adultery with her. She got pregnant and the king sent for her husband by name Uriah from the battlefield where he was fighting on behalf of Israel. The king thought that by bringing Uriah home, he would go home and spend time with Bathsheba. This way, the king's adultery would be kept secret and the pregnancy would be considered as being for Uriah. Uriah refused to go home to be with his wife and so the king plotted his death. These acts of adultery and murder triggered a series of events that begun to plague the king's reign including rape in the palace, mutiny and civil war.

Every individual, corporate entity or government that felt discontented during winter, often planned a way to increase their space. "Elisha died and was buried. Now Moabite raiders used to enter the country every spring." 2 Kings 13:20. Notice that at every season of Spring, these Moabites raided the land of Israel. Each year during winter, the enemy device plans to invade our spiritual, emotional and financial space, which they also execute during Spring.

Spiritual warfare is the highlight of the Spring season. This spiritual season is not necessarily scheduled to tally with the physical schedule of Spring. Our spiritual season of Spring is the divine schedule revealed to us by the Holy Spirit for us do warfare. Sometimes this schedule is revealed through the leadership of the local Church, and we must willingly oblige ourselves. Failure to engage the enemy in warfare may result in the loss of spiritual, emotional, and financial space to the enemy. Whenever we are convicted to engage in warfare, it is the Holy Spirit manifesting as the river Hiddekel to arm us to confront the enemy and take our space.

Summer: Summer is the season everyone looks forward to experience. People stay outdoors to enjoy the warmth of the beautiful weather. With several people scheduling their vacation during summer, the beaches are patronized with fun seekers. "The man brought me back to the entrance to the temple, and I saw water coming out from under the threshold of the temple toward the east (for the temple faced east). The water was coming down from under the south side of the temple, south of the altar. He then brought me out through the north gate and led me around the outside to the outer gate facing east, and the water was trickling from the south side. As the man went eastward with a measuring line in his hand, he measured off a thousand cubits and then led me through water that was ankle-deep. He measured off another thousand cubits and led me through water that was knee-deep. He measured off another thousand and led me through water that was up to the waist. He measured off another thousand, but now it was a river that I could not cross, because the water had risen and was deep enough to swim in—a river that no one could cross. He asked me, "Son of man, do you see this?"

Seed And Harvest In A Concurrent Era

Then he led me back to the bank of the river. When I arrived there, I saw a great number of trees on each side of the river. He said to me, "This water flows toward the eastern region and goes down into the Arabah, where it enters the Dead Sea. When it empties into the sea, the salty water there becomes fresh. Swarms of living creatures will live wherever the river flows. There will be large numbers of fish, because this water flows there and makes the salt water fresh; so where the river flows everything will live. Fishermen will stand along the shore; from En Gedi to En Eglaim there will be places for spreading nets. The fish will be of many kinds—like the fish of the Mediterranean Sea. But the swamps and marshes will not become fresh; they will be left for salt. Fruit trees of all kinds will grow on both banks of the river. Their leaves will not wither, nor will their fruit fail. Every month they will bear fruit, because the water from the sanctuary flows to them. Their fruit will serve for food and their leaves for healing." Ezekiel 47:1-12. Summer is the season for the manifestation of harvest. The seasons started out in Autumn where we are furnished with seed to cultivate our fields. The Holy Spirit streamed divine counsel through the river Pison and in this divine encounter of Ezekiel the prophet, it is described as ankle deep water that issued out of the sanctuary. A thousand cubits further away, this water becomes knee deep and is significant of Gihon, the river that flows during Winter. Another thousand cubits further away, the water from the sanctuary becomes waist deep and is significant of Hiddekel, the river that flows into our lives during Spring. Beyond this point, the water from the sanctuary is so deep, it requires one to swim through. This is the ministry of the Holy Spirit to the believer in their summer season. The river here is the Euphrates that is significant of abundance and enlargement. Four core manifestations at this point of the river from the Sanctuary require one to be a swimmer, healer, inherent leader, and fisherman.

Swimmer: Summer is the deep-water space of a mature swimmer. One must have the ability to swim and float in deep waters to access the fruitful trees situated at the banks of the river. The ripe fruits of a harvest are reaped through the maturity of the 'fruit of the Spirit' in the harvester. The 'fruit of the Spirit' constitute the promptings of the Holy Spirit by which the believer develops spiritual character. "The acts of the flesh are obvious: sexual immorality, impurity and debauchery; idolatry and witchcraft; hatred, discord, jealousy, fits of rage, selfish ambition, dissensions, factions and envy; drunkenness, orgies, and the like. I warn you, as I did before, that those who live like this will not inherit the kingdom of God. But the fruit of the Spirit is love, joy, peace, forbearance, kindness, goodness, faithfulness, gentleness and self-control. Against such things there is no law. Those who belong to Christ Jesus have crucified the flesh with its passions and desires. Since we live by the Spirit, let us keep in step with the Spirit. Let us not become conceited, provoking and envying each other."

Seed And Harvest In A Concurrent Era

Galatians 5:19-26. From the point when one gets saved, the indwelling Holy Spirit begins to prompt the believer to walk in the Spirit to overcome the various lusts of the flesh. Yielding ourselves to these promptings is how we become mature swimmers. "Wherefore seeing we also are compassed about with so great a cloud of witnesses, let us lay aside every weight, and the sin which doth so easily beset us, and let us run with patience the race that is set before us." Hebrews 12:1. During our summer season, people become attracted to the manifestation of the 'fruit of the Spirit' in our lives. Regrettably, such people may not know how to swim, so they gravitate toward us loaded heavily with the lusts of the flesh. However, a mature swimmer is capable of rescuing someone who is drowning in water so our mission during the summer is to rescue the perishing.

Healer: Our divine purpose is the conduit for divine healing. The seeds we are prompted to cultivate during the Autumn of our lives that survive the Winter and Spring seasons, produce healing leaves in the summer. "For the hurt of the daughter of my people am I hurt; I am black; astonishment hath taken hold on me. Is there no balm in Gilead; is there no physician there? why then is not the health of the daughter of my people recovered?" Jeremiah 8:21-22. Here, Israel is going through austere times and God's people are challenged in almost all areas of their lives. The question: "Is there no physician there" speaks to how God's people have persistently ignored the divinely appointed times scheduled for their transformation. The Sabbath, Passover, First-fruits, Pentecost, Trumpets, Atonement and Tabernacles were designed to bring a quickening to God's people. A believer whose spirit is quickened by the divine visitations of the appointed times becomes a physician. Regardless of what occupation is your divine purpose, God designed for us to be a channel of divine healing. Hence, one called as a lawyer is meant to be a conduit for legal healing, an engineer ought to be a conduit for technical healing etc. On the other hand, what we experience even today is that professionals in almost all arenas of life tend to oppress and exploit others. Without a transformation of the human spirit, one can never become the physician that God intended.

"Is there no balm in Gilead" is significant of the product or service that we render. A typical advertisement of medications on television would often mention so many possible side effects that it is often frightening. The reason is that over the years, those in the pharmaceutical as well as other industries masked the potential dangers associated with their products so the unsuspecting public became plagued in various ways. With profiteering as the core goal of professionals and entrepreneurs of our world, this tendency would continue to destroy us unabatedly. A genuine product or service must always heal even beyond what is advertised. The Summer season of the believer is when the products and services we render become the healing balm for our world.

Inherent Leader: The Summer season is when there is an abundance of food whether cultivated or naturally appearing. "Go to the ant, thou sluggard; consider her ways, and be wise: which having no guide, overseer, or ruler, provides her meat in the summer, and gathers her food in the harvest." Proverbs 6:6-8. The ant is a tiny and feeble creature that one can easily crush under the feet and yet displays phenomenal inherent leadership qualities. By exhibiting leadership qualities of a self-motivated overseer, guide and ruler, the ant compensates for its mediocre size and inadequacies.

Overseer – One who perceives a vision of destiny. Vision is a key leadership tool for the achievement of great exploits. My dad acquired a large parcel of land in the outskirts of the city where we resided. Usually during the summer, we would visit the land and cultivate tomatoes and other vegetables. There was a huge anthill on the property and my dad hired some laborers to destroy it. Interestingly, the following year in summer when we returned, there were three other huge anthills on the property. We were unable to win the war against these ants until we fully developed buildings on the property and inhabited it. "Where there is no revelation, people cast off restraint; but blessed is the one who heeds wisdom's instruction." Proverbs 29:18

(NIV). Though many confuse ambition for vision, vision is a revelation from God. It is a picture of one's destiny that is given supernaturally. Vision is not what great things we can achieve; rather it is where God intends for us to arrive when we diligently walk with Him.

Guide – This mean to break down the vision into various goals and objectives. This is the essence of planning. "I will stand my watch and set myself on the rampart and watch to see what He will say to me, and what I will answer when I am corrected. Then the Lord answered me and said: "Write the vision and make it plain on tablets, that he may run who reads it. For the vision is yet for an appointed time; but at the end it will speak, and it will not lie. Though it tarries, wait for it; because it will surely come, it will not tarry." Habakkuk 2:1-3. A vision is not a plan until it is documented with the facts of research and organized into goals and objectives. While some people craft a plan based on their own ambition, others receive a divine revelation of their destiny and yet fail to craft a comprehensive plan. All such people often end up disappointed. God told Habakkuk the prophet to write down the vision and make it plain on tables. A divine revelation of destiny requires a comprehensive plan of action. Goals must be ascertained through a feasibility study and objectives properly articulated. 'That he may run that reads it" is the strategic component of the plan. Strategy is how one engages resources to tackle an objective. It means that God is interested in deploying angels to provision your plan with people, opportunities, and resources. Any prudent professional or investor who would participate in your vision would also want to study the plan.

Ruler – One who governs with the divine principles for executing tasks. Paying close attention to these ants as children, we noticed that they would often form a line to move tiny food fragments each to store up in the anthill. The ants never broke their formation and when there was an obstacle in their path, they would often climb over the obstruction and continue in their lines. These ants operated as an army with obvious discipline. Objectives outlined in the comprehensive plan are executed as tasks. Each task requires a unique method. Methods are always based on sound rules or principles. Whenever we study or listen to God's word, He convicts us with divine principles to furnish us with the right methods for specific tasks in our plan. He would continue to help us reshape the plan until it becomes the blueprint for our prosperity. Joseph knew what method would help Egypt overcome the impending famine that was revealed in a dream to Pharaoh. He prescribed that a fifth of the harvest during the years of abundance be stored up against the seven years of famine and this alleviated Egypt from the devastation of a famine.

Fisherman: The river Euphrates, which is also the overwhelming waters from the sanctuary that flows to the

Seed And Harvest In A Concurrent Era

believer during the summer season of harvest, is full of
fishes. "Fishermen will stand along the shore; from En
Gedi to En Eglaim there will be places for spreading nets."
Fishermen deploy baits and nets for their catch. "One day
as Jesus was standing by the Lake of Gennesaret, the people
were crowding around him and listening to the word of
God. He saw at the lake's edge two boats, left there by the
fishermen, who were washing their nets. He got into one of
the boats, the one belonging to Simon, and asked him to
put out a little from shore. Then he sat down and taught the
people from the boat. When he had finished speaking, he
said to Simon, "Put out into deep water, and let down the
nets for a catch." Simon answered, "Master, we've worked
hard all night and haven't caught anything. But because you
say so, I will let down the nets." When they had done so,
they caught such a large number of fish that their nets began
to break. So they signaled their partners in the other boat
to come and help them, and they came and filled both boats
so full that they began to sink. When Simon Peter saw this,
he fell at Jesus' knees and said, "Go away from me, Lord; I
am a sinful man!" For he and all his companions were
astonished at the catch of fish they had taken, and so were
James and John, the sons of Zebedee, Simon's partners.
Then Jesus said to Simon, "Don't be afraid; from now on
you will fish for people." So they pulled their boats up on
shore, left everything and followed him." Luke 5:1-11. Jesus
needed a platform to preach the gospel and asked Simon a
fisherman to avail his boat. Simon had tried unsuccessfully

to catch fish for an entire night. After Jesus had used his boat to minister to the people, He instructed Simon to launch the nets for a catch. Simon initially protested but then yielded to the instruction. To his amazement he caught so many fishes that he had to seek the help of other fishermen to haul in the harvest.

The Bait - What Simon did not realize was that the boat he yielded for Jesus as a platform to preach the gospel was a supernatural bait. A bait is used to attract fishes to the location of fishermen. The bait is the seed for harvest. During the season of harvest, the Holy Spirit flowing as Euphrates prompts us to sow certain seeds that serve as a bait for the harvest.

The Net - A harvest of fishes is significant of souls. "Again, the kingdom of heaven is like unto a net, that was cast into the sea, and gathered of every kind: which, when it was full, they drew to shore, and sat down, and gathered the good into vessels, but cast the bad away." Matthew 13:47,48. There is a specific kind of harvest that is beneficial to our mission. Fishermen often go fishing with a mission to catch a specific kind of fish. Usually this is at the request of their clients who often pay an advance to sponsor the fishing voyage. The fishermen would equip themselves with the right kind of nets to catch such fish. For instance, if they went out seeking salmon fishes, they would ignore a school of shrimp that come their way. The nets for catching salmon would be highly inappropriate to catch shrimp. Usually when a harvest is hauled into the boat, it may be mixed with some other kind of fishes but the diligence of fishing is to throw those back into the water. In the season of harvest, there is a tendency that our bait may attract all kinds of people and yet it is essential that we remain mission oriented on who we keep. Not everyone has a place in our destiny and so whoever we are prompted not to keep must not be given a permanent place.

CHAPTER THREE

THE KAIROS

The 'Chronos' and 'Kairos' are two Greek words that show how time is determined. While 'Chronos' is a succession of moments measured by length, 'Kairos' means an opportune time. Chronos is how we determine time as twenty-four in a day, seven days a week, twelve months in a year. A child in elementary school learns this basic of time. Often, we become fixated on our age and by comparing with contemporaries, we gauge what we ought to have accomplished. Some people end up depressed or may even commit suicide assuming they feel frustrated with their accomplishments. The Kairos is the opportune time for everything. Significant manifestations, major changes, great promotions are divinely ordained opportune times. There is no fixed age where a person must experience significant promotion or a major change in their lifetime. However, there are three factors that determine the Kairos and these are generational, ancestral, prophetic covenant time factors. Unlike the Chronos which is a single-finger timer that is configured to measure time as predictable moments, the Kairos is a three-finger timer. The generational, ancestral, and prophetic covenant time factors are the fingers of the Kairos timer. These three factors exert either a push forward or pull backwards on the Kairos timer when it is set.

Generational Time Factor

The generational time factor is the gauge of our alignment or defiance of the scriptures. This is a scale by which our righteousness is measured versus iniquity. God Almighty is the judge of the whole earth, and He executes judgements that determine the fate of the righteous and unrighteous. In Psalms 75 the scriptures record: "We praise you, God, we praise you, for your Name is near; people tell of your wonderful deeds. You say, "I choose the appointed time; it is I who judge with equity. When the earth and all its people quake, it is I who hold its pillars firm. To the arrogant I say, 'Boast no more,' and to the wicked, 'Do not lift up your horns. Do not lift your horns against heaven; do not speak so defiantly.'" No one from the east or the west or from the desert can exalt themselves. It is God who judges: He brings one down, he exalts another. In the hand of the Lord is a cup full of foaming wine mixed with spices; he pours it out, and all the wicked of the earth drink it down to its very dregs. As for me, I will declare this forever; I will sing praise to the God of Jacob, who says, "I will cut off the horns of all the wicked, but the horns of the righteous will be lifted up."

People often wonder why those who are wicked in society seem to continue in their ways unabated. The generational factor of the Kairos is usually a long span of time, and the following encounter of Abraham unfolds this truth. "After this, the word of the Lord came to Abram in a vision: "Do not be afraid, Abram. I am your shield, your very great reward." But Abram said, "Sovereign Lord, what can you give me since I remain childless and the one who will inherit my estate is Eliezer of Damascus?" And Abram said, "You have given me no children; so a servant in my household will be my heir." Then the word of the Lord came to him: "This man will not be your heir, but a son who is your own flesh and blood will be your heir." He took him outside and said, "Look up at the sky and count the stars—if indeed you can count them." Then he said to him, "So shall your offspring be." Abram believed the Lord, and he credited it to him as righteousness. He also said to him, "I am the Lord, who brought you out of Ur of the Chaldeans to give you this land to take possession of it." But Abram said, "Sovereign Lord, how can I know that I will gain possession of it?" So the Lord said to him, "Bring me a heifer, a goat and a ram, each three years old, along with a dove and a young pigeon." Abram brought all these to him, cut them in two and arranged the halves opposite each other; the birds, however, he did not cut in half. Then birds of prey came down on the carcasses, but Abram drove them away. As the sun was setting, Abram fell into a deep sleep, and a thick and dreadful darkness came over him. Then the Lord said to him, "Know for certain that for four hundred years your descendants will be strangers in a country not their own and that they will be enslaved and mistreated there. But I will punish the nation they serve as slaves, and afterward they will come out with great possessions. You, however, will go to your ancestors in peace and be buried at a good old age. In the fourth generation your descendants will come back here, for the sin of the Amorites has not yet reached its full measure." Genesis 15:1-16

Abraham had been called by God to pilgrimage in the land of Canaan. At this point Abraham had no child with his wife Sarah so he was concerned. God assured Abraham of a biological offspring through a covenant where God allured to some significant specifics. "Know for certain that for four hundred years your descendants will be strangers in a country not their own and that they will be enslaved and mistreated there. But I will punish the nation they serve as slaves, and afterward they will come out with great possessions. You, however, will go to your ancestors in peace and be buried at a good old age. In the fourth generation your descendants will come back here, for the sin of the Amorites has not yet reached its full measure." For four hundred years, the descendants of Abraham will be enslaved in a strange land. The fourth generation of these descendants of Abraham will emigrate from this strange land with wealth. Meanwhile the reason the descendants of Abraham cannot inherit the land of the Canaanites before the period stated is that the iniquity of the present occupants of the land has not yet measured up to the degree that disenfranchises them of legitimate ownership.

"When the earth and all its people quake, it is I who hold its pillars firm." Psalms 75:3. The function of God as judge of the earth is how He exercises the premise for the tranquility of the elements. Four hundred years also regarded as four generations is quite a long time for the wicked to continue in their evil ways. However, this is the attribute of God known as longsuffering. "Then the Lord came down in the cloud and stood there with him and proclaimed his name, the Lord. And he passed in front of Moses, proclaiming, "The Lord, the Lord, the compassionate and gracious God, slow to anger, abounding in love and faithfulness, maintaining love to thousands, and forgiving wickedness, rebellion and sin. Yet he does not leave the guilty unpunished; he punishes the children and their children for the sin of the parents to the third and fourth generation." Exodus 34:5-7. Notice that in this encounter of Moses where God manifested His glory, the divine attribute of rendering punishment to those who continue in iniquity is unveiled with this same timeframe of four generations.

Process of Time - The fourth generation of the Israelites who were in Egypt became agitated by their sufferings of the Pharaoh's oppression. "Now it happened in the process of time that the king of Egypt died. Then the children of Israel groaned because of the bondage, and they cried out; and their cry came up to God because of the bondage. So God heard their groaning, and God remembered His covenant with Abraham, with Isaac, and with Jacob. And God looked upon the children of Israel, and God acknowledged them." Exodus 2:23-25. The process of time signals when the fourth-generation count is up. The longsuffering time limit for God's tolerance of iniquity against the oppressed triggers an agitation in their hearts. This is the point where we either turn to the occult or to God for salvation. Cain and Abel suffered the consequence of the sin of their parents until the longsuffering time limit of the process of time. "And in the process of time it came to pass that Cain brought an offering of the fruit of the ground to the Lord. Abel also brought of the firstborn of his flock and of their fat. And the Lord respected Abel and his offering, but He did not respect Cain and his offering. And Cain was very angry, and his countenance fell. So the Lord said to Cain, "Why are you angry? And why has your countenance fallen? If you do well, will you not be accepted? And if you do not do well, sin lies at the door. And its desire is for you, but you should rule over it." Genesis 4:3-7. The process of time describes that point when God points man to salvation so that his oppression comes to an end. This is the point when God inspired Cain and Abel to offer up a sacrifice. Notice that though Cain failed to offer up an acceptable sacrifice, God reached out to him and admonished that he should do the right thing. The heartbeat of God yearns for our salvation in the process of time.

Salvation through Christ Jesus is the only escape for the descendants of workers of iniquity who are being weighed in scales of the fourth-generation count. "But when the kindness and love of God our Savior appeared, he saved us, not because of righteous things we had done, but because of his mercy. He saved us through the washing of rebirth and renewal by the Holy Spirit, whom he poured out on us generously through Jesus Christ our Savior, so that, having been justified by his grace, we might become heirs having the hope of eternal life." Titus 3:4-7. For those who have accepted Jesus Christ as their Lord and Savior the fourth-generation punishment is abated. The 'washing of regeneration' is the impact that God's word makes on the believer. "... just as Christ also loved the church and gave Himself for her, that He might sanctify and cleanse her with the washing of water by the word, that He might present her to Himself a glorious church, not having spot or wrinkle or any such thing, but that she should be holy and without blemish." Ephesians 5:25b-27. The word of God continually convicting the believer to live a righteous life washes like water, and removes the spots, wrinkles, and blemishes of sin. Through salvation we become regenerated in Christ. "But you are a chosen generation, a royal priesthood, a holy nation, His own special people, that you may proclaim the praises of Him who called you out of darkness into His marvelous light; who once were not a people but are now the people of God, who had not obtained mercy but now have obtained mercy." 1 Peter 2:9,10. Salvation is an awesome change of status for the new believer in Christ. The generational time clock is set to zero for the believer who is now yielded to the righteousness of God in Christ Jesus. Old things are passed away and all things are made new in Christ Jesus our Lord and Savior. It is a new beginning and for no reason should we allow that old clock to rewind itself. We become the new standard for the Kairos timer which is a scale that measures our righteousness against the unrighteousness of the wicked. While the washing of regeneration is regenerating us, the degeneration of the wicked continues unabated. As the washing of regeneration undo our spots, wrinkles, and blemishes our spiritual weight is measured against the degeneration of the wicked. The paradigm shift of wealth transfer becomes due for the righteous at the point when their righteousness becomes weightier than the wicked. Jesus said in Matthew 5:20: "For I say to you, that unless your righteousness exceeds the righteousness of the scribes and Pharisees, you will by no means enter the kingdom of heaven."

Joshua led the Israelites that came out of Egypt to conquer and settle in the Promised Land. After about four generations, Israel defaulted in Sabbath land rests to the amount of seventy years. "Therefore He brought against them the king of the Chaldeans, who killed their young men with the sword in the house of their sanctuary, and had no compassion on young man or virgin, on the aged or the weak; He gave them all into his hand. And all the articles from the house of God, great and small, the treasures of the house of the Lord, and the treasures of the king and of his leaders, all these he took to Babylon. Then they burned the house of God, broke down the wall of Jerusalem, burned all its palaces with fire, and destroyed all its precious possessions. And those who escaped from the sword he carried away to Babylon, where they became servants to him and his sons until the rule of the kingdom of Persia, to fulfill the word of the Lord by the mouth of Jeremiah, until the land had enjoyed her Sabbaths. As long as she lay desolate she kept Sabbath, to fulfill seventy years." 2 Chronicles 36:17-21. King Nebuchadnezzar was empowered by God to conquer Israel and take them into captivity. Those who heard Jeremiah the prophet speak of the impending captivity did not receive his words and the prophet suffered character assassination and imprisonment by the rulers of his day. Eventually, the Israelites were taken into captivity by King Nebuchadnezzar. While Israel was in the captivity of Babylon, there was an occasion where the heir of King Nebuchadnezzar saw a hand writing on the walls of his palace: "Belshazzar the king made a great feast for a thousand of his lords, and drank wine in the presence of the thousand. While he tasted the wine, Belshazzar gave the command to bring the gold and silver vessels which his father Nebuchadnezzar had taken from the temple which had been in Jerusalem, that the king and his lords, his wives, and his concubines might drink from them. Then they brought the gold vessels that had been taken from the temple of the house of God which had been in Jerusalem; and the king and his lords, his wives, and his concubines drank from them. They drank wine, and praised the gods of gold and silver, bronze and iron, wood and stone. In the same hour the fingers of a man's hand appeared and wrote opposite the lampstand on the plaster of the wall of the king's palace; and the king saw the part of the hand that wrote. Then the king's countenance changed, and his thoughts troubled him, so that the joints of his hips were loosened and his knees knocked against each other. The king cried aloud to bring in the astrologers, the Chaldeans, and the soothsayers. The king spoke, saying to the wise men of Babylon, "Whoever reads this writing, and tells me its interpretation, shall be clothed with purple and have a chain of gold around his neck; and he shall be the third ruler in the kingdom." Now all the king's wise men came, but they could not read the writing, or make known to the king its interpretation. Then King Belshazzar was greatly troubled, his countenance was changed, and his lords were astonished. The queen, because of the words of the king and his lords, came to the banquet hall. The queen spoke, saying, "O king, live forever! Do not let your thoughts trouble you, nor let your countenance change. There is a man in your kingdom in whom is the Spirit of the Holy God. And in the days of your father, light and understanding and wisdom, like the wisdom of the gods, were found in him; and King Nebuchadnezzar your father—your father the king—made him chief of the magicians, astrologers, Chaldeans, and soothsayers. Inasmuch as an excellent spirit, knowledge, understanding, interpreting dreams, solving riddles, and explaining enigmas were found in this Daniel, whom the king named Belteshazzar, now let Daniel be called, and he will give the interpretation." ... "Then Daniel answered, and said before the king, "Let your gifts be for yourself, and give your rewards to another; yet I will read the writing to the king, and make known to him the interpretation. O king, the Most High God gave Nebuchadnezzar your father a kingdom and majesty, glory and honor. And because of the majesty that He gave him, all peoples, nations, and languages trembled and feared before him. Whomever he wished, he executed; whomever he wished, he kept alive; whomever he wished, he set up; and whomever he wished, he put down. But when his heart was lifted up, and his spirit was hardened in pride, he was deposed from his kingly throne, and they took his glory from him. Then he was driven from the sons of men, his heart was made like the beasts, and his dwelling was with the wild donkeys. They fed him with grass like oxen, and his body was wet with the dew of heaven, till he knew that the Most High God rules in the kingdom of men, and appoints over it whomever He chooses. "But you his son, Belshazzar, have not humbled your heart, although you knew all this. And you have [m]lifted yourself up against the Lord of heaven. They have brought the vessels of His house before you, and you and your lords, your wives and your concubines, have drunk wine from them. And you have praised the gods of silver and gold, bronze and iron, wood and stone, which do not see or hear or know; and the God who holds your breath in His hand and owns all your ways, you have not glorified. Then the fingers of the hand were sent from Him, and this writing was written. "And this is the inscription that was written: MENE, MENE, TEKEL, UPHARSIN. This is the interpretation of each word. MENE: God has numbered your kingdom, and finished it; TEKEL: You have been weighed in the balances, and found wanting; PERES: Your kingdom has been divided, and given to the Medes and Persians." Then Belshazzar gave the command, and they clothed Daniel with purple and put a chain of gold around his neck and made a proclamation concerning him that he should be the third ruler in the kingdom. That very night Belshazzar, king of the Chaldeans, was slain. And Darius the Mede received the kingdom, being about sixty-two years old." Daniel 5.

The scale of divine judgment weighs everyone regardless of religion, race or gender. Scriptural truths are the standard for this scale. In the same way Israel was judged and subdued into captivity, the successive ruler of Babylon was also judged and lost his life as well as the reign of his kingdom. At every point, we are either degenerating or being regenerated. If we are degenerating, then we are headed for a judgment of demotion. However, if we are basking in the washing of regeneration that is accorded believers in Christ, the clock is now ticking towards a judgment of promotion.

Ancestral Time Factor

The ancestral time factor of the Kairos is the gauge of our alignment or defiance of divine purpose. Often, the word 'purpose' is used casually in society to describe our passions or whatever we have great energy to pursue. While passion is the invigorating fuel that sustains the pursuit of purpose and is one component of purpose, divine purpose is an interface that also consists of revelations and burdens. Without any one of these components, purpose falls short. Divine purpose is the ancestral time factor that measures us on the scales of the Kairos timer. Whenever we come into God's presence, we are weighed on the scales of the Kairos timer. "When I shall receive the congregation, I will judge uprightly." Psalm 75:2. God's people congregate at the 'appointed times' of Sabbath, Passover, First-fruits, Pentecost, Trumpets, Atonement and Tabernacles. Whenever we come into God's presence, he weighs us against the wicked and amends us through conviction. Divine purpose carves out unique wilderness trials that fosters our intercessory mandate.

Wilderness Trials – There is a spiritual time frame of forty days where we ought to overcome 'self'. The attributes of 'self' include fear, inferiority complex, greed, complaining and murmuring. 'Self' is the nature of sin in us, and Satan is its advocate. He lured Eve in the Garden of Eden to succumb to 'self' and so the entire human race is infected with this core vice. Jesus said in Mark 8:34: "When He had called the people to Himself, with His disciples also, He said to them, "Whoever desires to come after Me, let him deny himself, and take up his cross, and follow Me." Self-denial is core to the gospel message. Salvation entails self-denial to carry the burden of our cross. Our Lord Jesus assigns a cross to everyone who follows Him. This cross is the burden of divine purpose by which we overcome the three types of sin. "For all that is in the world—the lust of the flesh, the lust of the eyes, and the pride of life—is not of the Father but is of the world." 1 John 2:16. Lust of the flesh, lust of the eyes and pride of life are the ways by which the devil enslaves us to the sinful nature of 'self'.

Seed And Harvest In A Concurrent Era

Throughout the scriptures we find instances where those who were used mightily of God had to be purged of 'self'.

Joseph was the descendant of Abraham who took the lead into Egypt as God had indicated in the covenant with Abraham. "He sent a man before them—Joseph—who was sold as a slave. They hurt his feet with fetters, He was laid in irons. Until the time that his word came to pass, the word of the Lord tested him. The king sent and released him, the ruler of the people let him go free. He made him lord of his house, and ruler of all his possessions, to bind his princes at his pleasure, and teach his elders wisdom. Psalms 105:17-22. At the age of seventeen, Joseph received revelations that meant he would become a prominent person in the future. His brothers hated him for his dreams and sold him to become a slave in Egypt. An Egyptian by name Potiphar bought Joseph. Interestingly, Joseph kept devotion to God and was not depressed by his condition of slavery. "Now Joseph had been taken down to Egypt. And Potiphar, an officer of Pharaoh, captain of the guard, an Egyptian, bought him from the Ishmaelites who had taken him down there. The Lord was with Joseph, and he was a successful man; and he was in the house of his master the Egyptian. And his master saw that the Lord was with him and that the Lord made all he did to prosper in his hand. So Joseph found favor in his sight, and served him. Then he made him overseer of his house, and all that he had he put under his authority. So it was, from the time that he had made him overseer of his house and all that he had, that the Lord blessed the Egyptian's house for Joseph's sake; and the blessing of the Lord was on all that he had in the house and in the field. Thus he left all that he had in Joseph's hand, and he did not know what he had except for the bread which he ate." Genesis 39:1-6. Here, we see that Joseph quickly masters his environment and the presence of God distinguishes and elevates him. Joseph is promoted to chief steward of Potiphar's estate. This is his mastery over the 'lust of the eyes'. While working in Potiphar's house, the wife of Potiphar attempted to indulge Joseph in sexual sin unsuccessfully and accused Joseph of attempted rape. Though this incident led to the imprisonment of Joseph, it was his moment of mastery over the 'lust of the flesh'. Thirteen years after the dream he had at the age seventeen, Joseph was made Prime Minister of Egypt. The scripture says that the word of God tested him. This means that the revelation of purpose orchestrated the trials that Joseph went through. "The words of the Lord are pure words, like silver tried in a furnace of earth, purified seven times." Psalms 12:6. God's revelation of purpose to us orchestrates wilderness trials for us. Joseph was promoted to Prime Minister of Egypt when he passed the test. This was evidence of his mastery of the 'pride of life'. We see evidence that he became purged of self when his brothers, fearing that Joseph would retribute them for their hatred sought his forgiveness. "Joseph said to them, "Do not be afraid, for am I in the place of God? But as for you, you meant evil against me; but God meant it for good, in order to bring it about as it is this day, to save many people alive." Genesis 50:19,20. After going through the wilderness of trials, Joseph was purged of 'self' and so was not bitter against his brothers.

According to God's covenant, the descendants of Abraham would be in the strange land that is Egypt for four generations. Moses was a part of the fourth generation. "He sent Moses His servant, and Aaron whom He had chosen. They performed His signs among them, and wonders in the land of Ham. He sent darkness, and made it dark; and they did not rebel against His word. He turned their waters into blood, and killed their fish. Their land abounded with frogs, even in the chambers of their kings. He spoke, and there came swarms of flies, and lice in all their territory. He gave them hail for rain, and flaming fire in their land. He struck their vines also, and their fig trees, and splintered the trees of their territory. He spoke, and locusts came, young locusts without number, and ate up all the vegetation in their land, and devoured the fruit of their ground. He also destroyed all the firstborn in their land, the first of all their strength. He also brought them out with silver and gold, and there was none feeble among His tribes. Egypt was glad when they departed, for the fear of them had fallen upon them. He spread a cloud for a covering, and fire to give light in the night. The people asked, and He brought quail, and satisfied them with the bread of heaven. He opened the rock, and water gushed out; it ran in the dry places like a river. For He remembered His holy promise, and Abraham His servant." Psalm 105:26-42. Moses received revelation of purpose to secure the release of the Israelites from Egypt. When Moses confronted the Pharaoh of Egypt to do so, the Pharaoh refused to grant the request of Moses. It took ten plagues invoked by Moses against Egypt to secure the release of the Israelites. During this time of the plagues, the Pharaoh increased oppression against the Israelites to frustrate the intentions of Moses. However, the Israelites endured with Moses and when the Pharaoh released the Israelites, there was a great transfer of the possessions of the Egyptians to the Israelites. This was Israel's mastery of the 'lust of the eyes'. While in the wilderness away from Egypt, God simulated an environment of trials intended to purge the Israelites of 'self'. Moses recounts in Deuteronomy 8:1-5: "Every commandment which I command you today you must be careful to observe, that you may live and multiply, and go in and possess the land of which the Lord swore to your fathers. And you shall remember that the Lord your God led you all the way these forty years in the wilderness, to humble you and test you, to know what was in your heart, whether you would keep His commandments or not. So He humbled you, allowed you to hunger, and fed you with manna which you did not know nor did your fathers know, that He might make you know that man shall not live by bread alone; but man lives by every word that proceeds from the mouth of the Lord. Your garments did not wear out on you, nor did your foot swell these forty years. You should know in your heart that as a man chastens his son, so the Lord your God chastens you." The need of the Israelites for the basic necessities of life such as water and food were a divine orchestration to test how they would conduct themselves. Unfortunately, they murmured and complained whenever there was a need and so they consistently failed the test of the 'lust of the flesh'. Interestingly, at every such instance, Moses would seek God and their need would be met. At the threshold of the Promised Land, twelve tribal leaders were sent to conduct a feasibility study. They returned after forty days with evidence of the riches of the Promised Land. Ten of these tribal leaders discouraged the congregation concerning the nature of the occupants of the land and this triggered widespread murmuring against Moses and God. Joshua and Caleb were the only two tribal leaders who trusted that God was able to help Israel conquer the Promised Land. As a result of the widespread murmuring, God told the Israelites to return to the wilderness. "According to the number of the days in which you spied out the land, forty days, for each day you shall bear your guilt one year, namely forty years, and you shall know My rejection. I the Lord have spoken this. I will surely do so to all this evil congregation who are gathered together against Me. In this wilderness they shall be consumed, and there they shall die.'" Numbers 14:34.35. An entire generation failed the wilderness test of the 'pride of life' and so a journey of forty days became forty years of death in the wilderness. It was an entirely new generation of Israelites together with Caleb, that Joshua led to conquer the Promised Land.

Our Lord Jesus Christ also went through forty days of wilderness trials. "Then Jesus was led up by the Spirit into the wilderness to be tempted by the devil. And when He had fasted forty days and forty nights, afterward He was hungry. Now when the tempter came to Him, he said, "If You are the Son of God, command that these stones become bread." But He answered and said, "It is written, 'Man shall not live by bread alone, but by every word that proceeds from the mouth of God.'" Then the devil took Him up into the holy city, set Him on the pinnacle of the temple, and said to Him, "If You are the Son of God, throw Yourself down. For it is written: 'He shall give His angels charge over you,' and, 'In their hands they shall bear you up, Lest you dash your foot against a stone.'" Jesus said to him, "It is written again, 'You shall not tempt the Lord your God.'" Again, the devil took Him up on an exceedingly high mountain, and showed Him all the kingdoms of the world and their glory. And he said to Him, "All these things I will give You if You will fall down and worship me." Then Jesus said to him, "Away with you, Satan! For it is written, 'You shall worship the Lord your God, and Him only you shall serve.'" Then the devil left Him, and behold, angels came and ministered to Him. Matthew 4:1-11. While He was baptized by John, the heavens opened and there was a revelation that declared Jesus Christ as the Son of God. Immediately after this, he was led to fast for forty days and forty nights in the wilderness where He was tempted by the devil. Jesus was hungry and the devil suggested to command stones to turn into bread. He did not succumb to this temptation. The devil showed him all the material riches of the world and sought the worship of Jesus in exchange. Jesus refused this offer. The devil then led Jesus to the pinnacle of the temple and suggested that Jesus jump down since there was a scripture that promised that God would give the angels charge so that none of His feet would break. The motive behind this temptation was to lure Jesus to create a spectacle where all those at the temple would see Him jump that height and yet not get hurt. This temptation would have removed any doubt that He was the promised Messiah. Assuming Jesus succumbed to this temptation, the religious leaders would have wholehearted accepted and not crucified Jesus. However, this was not God's plan, so Jesus refused the bait. The plan of God was for Jesus to go to the cross and defeat the devil.

Intercessory Mandate – Running through our blood line from our great ancestors Adam and Eve are various attributes of 'self'. The pursuit of 'self' is a perversion that results in various ancestral ruins. These ancestral ruins manifest as chronic infirmities, desolations, and dysfunctions. "Those from among you shall build the old waste places; you shall raise up the foundations of many generations; and you shall be called the Repairer of the Breach, the Restorer of Streets to Dwell In." Isaiah 58:12. Divine purpose is intended to groom us into intercessors. Though many of us think of an intercessor as one who is passionate to pray for others, this is only one of the three components of purpose. Our wilderness trials unleashes God's grace to overcome 'self' so we can repair ancestral ruins. The cross of our Lord Jesus Christ was the bridge for peace between God and man. Similarly, when we embrace the cross of wilderness trials that God simulates for us, we overcome 'self' to become the bridge that streams the blood of Jesus to heal chronic diseases as well as fix serial desolations and dysfunctions of our families and society. We identify a simulated wilderness when the chosen environment of God for us to live or work triggers a lot of trials. This wilderness environment is designed to last for a spiritual forty-day period. However, this trial could practically last for just forty seconds or minutes or hours or days or weeks or months or years. The wilderness is intended to gauge our attitude in the face of our basic needs, material wants and status of life. One who trusts God wholeheartedly does not grumble, murmur, complain and is never arrogant, self-centered, or greedy.

Prophetic Covenant Factor

The prophetic covenant time factor of the Kairos is the gauge of our alignment or defiance of the anointing of the Holy Spirit. Gilgal, Bethel, Jericho, and the Jordan are four prophetic landmarks, which serve as reference point encounters of the Abrahamic covenant. "Christ has redeemed us from the curse of the law, having become a curse for us (for it is written, "Cursed is everyone who hangs on a tree"), that the blessing of Abraham might come upon the Gentiles in Christ Jesus, that we might receive the promise of the Spirit through faith." Galatians 3:13,14. Every destiny promise of God to us believers is predicated upon the Abrahamic covenant. Through His sacrifice on the cross, the Lord Jesus Christ grants us access to this overarching covenant, and the Holy Spirit through the anointing, facilitates our competence. 2 Kings 2:1-15 records this instance: "And it came to pass, when the Lord was about to take up Elijah into heaven by a whirlwind, that Elijah went with Elisha from Gilgal. Then Elijah said to Elisha, "Stay here, please, for the Lord has sent me on to Bethel." But Elisha said, "As the Lord lives, and as your soul lives, I will not leave you!" So they went down to Bethel. Now the sons of the prophets who were at Bethel came out to Elisha, and said to him, "Do you know that the Lord will take away your master from over you today?" And he said, "Yes, I know; keep silent!" Then Elijah said to him, "Elisha, stay here, please, for the Lord has sent me on to Jericho." But he said, "As the Lord lives, and as your soul lives, I will not leave you!" So they came to Jericho. Now the sons of the prophets who were at Jericho came to Elisha and said to him, "Do you know that the Lord will take away your master from over you today?" So he answered, "Yes,

I know; keep silent!" Then Elijah said to him, "Stay here, please, for the Lord has sent me on to the Jordan." But he said, "As the Lord lives, and as your soul lives, I will not leave you!" So the two of them went on. And fifty men of the sons of the prophets went and stood facing them at a distance, while the two of them stood by the Jordan. Now Elijah took his mantle, rolled it up, and struck the water; and it was divided this way and that, so that the two of them crossed over on dry ground. And so it was, when they had crossed over, that Elijah said to Elisha, "Ask! What may I do for you, before I am taken away from you?" Elisha said, "Please let a double portion of your spirit be upon me." So he said, "You have asked a hard thing. Nevertheless, if you see me when I am taken from you, it shall be so for you; but if not, it shall not be so." Then it happened, as they continued on and talked, that suddenly a chariot of fire appeared with horses of fire, and separated the two of them; and Elijah went up by a whirlwind into heaven. And Elisha saw it, and he cried out, "My father, my father, the chariot of Israel and its horsemen!" So he saw him no more. And he took hold of his own clothes and tore them into two pieces. He also took up the mantle of Elijah that had fallen from him, and went back and stood by the bank of the Jordan. Then he took the mantle of Elijah that had fallen from him, and struck the water, and said, "Where is the Lord God of Elijah?" And when he also had struck the water, it was divided this way and that; and Elisha crossed over. Now when the sons of the prophets who were from

Seed And Harvest In A Concurrent Era

Jericho saw him, they said, "The spirit of Elijah rests on Elisha." And they came to meet him and bowed to the ground before him.". On the day that Elijah was translated into the heavens, his protégé Elisha was to take over the ministry and function in this anointing. The anointing is not a random patchwork of Holy Spirit promptings that lack structure. Elisha needed to experience the landmark encounters at Gilgal, Bethel, Jericho, and Jordan as reference points of the anointing.

Gilgal - This is the landmark and reference point encounter for sanctification. Here, the regeneration of the believer is weighed against the degeneration of unbelievers. Gilgal is a method of the Holy Spirit anointing that indulges our regeneration. "At that time the Lord said to Joshua, "Make flint knives for yourself, and circumcise the sons of Israel again the second time." So Joshua made flint knives for himself, and circumcised the sons of Israel at the hill of the foreskins. And this is the reason why Joshua circumcised them: All the people who came out of Egypt who were males, all the men of war, had died in the wilderness on the way, after they had come out of Egypt. For all the people who came out had been circumcised, but all the people born in the wilderness, on the way as they came out of Egypt, had not been circumcised. For the children of Israel walked forty years in the wilderness, till all the people who were men of war, who came out of Egypt, were consumed, because they did not obey the voice of the Lord—to whom the Lord swore that He would not show them the land which the Lord had sworn to their fathers that He would give us, "a land flowing with milk and honey." Then Joshua circumcised their sons whom He raised up in their place; for they were uncircumcised, because they had not been circumcised on the way. So it was, when they had finished circumcising all the people, that they stayed in their places in the camp till they were healed. Then the Lord said to Joshua, "This day I have rolled away the reproach of Egypt from you." Therefore the name of the place is called Gilgal to this day." Joshua 5:2-9. Circumcision and sanctification are synonymous in the scriptures as they serve the same purpose. The origin of circumcision is the Abrahamic covenant where God required that Abraham and all his male descendants be circumcised on the eighth day after birth. It was the essence of sanctification in the descendants of Abraham for which there was no room for compromise. When Moses ignored to circumcise his son while he was on the journey to fulfil the divine assignment to deliver the Israelites out of Egypt, and it was passed the eighth day, he almost lost his life. "And it came to pass by the way in the inn, that the Lord met him, and sought to kill him. Then Zipporah took a sharp stone, and cut off the foreskin of her son, and cast it at his feet, and said, Surely a bloody husband art thou to me. So he let him go: then she said, A bloody husband thou art, because of the circumcision." Exodus 4:24-26. It is interesting how God who sent Moses could turn against him for violating the circumcision requirement.

Seed And Harvest In A Concurrent Era

Circumcision rolls away reproach from our spirit. Reproach is anything that causes shame and prevents the manifestation of the glory of God in our lives. Though circumcision was a requirement of the males, it is interesting to note that it was carried out by the women as in the case of Zipporah. It was a bloody experience to cut off the foreskin of an eight-year-old child. It left a lasting impression on those who experienced or saw the process. "For thus says the Lord to the men of Judah and Jerusalem: "Break up your fallow ground, and do not sow among thorns. Circumcise yourselves to the Lord, and take away the foreskins of your hearts, you men of Judah and inhabitants of Jerusalem, lest My fury come forth like fire, and burn so that no one can quench it, because of the evil of your doings." Jeremiah 4:3,4. Through divine revelation, Jeremiah the prophet compares circumcision with the agricultural processes of plowing and harrowing where weeds are dug out and removed from a farmland prior to sowing seeds. He then conveys the spiritual relevance as taking away the 'foreskins of the heart'. It is the uprooting of stubbornness that often stands in the way of our repentance. Every assignment that entails the anointing requires some form of sanctification. Sanctification brings the Abrahamic covenant requirement of circumcision to bear upon our works. In the same way that circumcision transitioned the name of Abram meaning 'exalted father' to Abraham 'father of many nations', circumcision is the divine token that indulges the anointing into our methods of work. Any process, formula, equation that lacks some form of circumcision is short of the anointing and so will become redundant with time. In the divine scheme to make Abraham fruitful, he needed to have a Gilgal experience. It was at this encounter that God specified when Isaac would be born.

Bethel - This is the landmark and reference point encounter of the house of God. It is a measure of our appointed time devotion as against heathen irreverence. Bethel is a method of the Holy Spirit anointing that indulges reverence. "Now Jacob went out from Beersheba and went toward Haran. So he came to a certain place and stayed there all night, because the sun had set. And he took one of the stones of that place and put it at his head, and he lay down in that place to sleep. Then he dreamed, and behold, a ladder was set up on the earth, and its top reached to heaven; and there the angels of God were ascending and descending on it. And behold, the Lord stood above it and said: "I am the Lord God of Abraham your father and the God of Isaac; the land on which you lie I will give to you and your descendants. Also your descendants shall be as the dust of the earth; you shall spread abroad to the west and the east, to the north and the south; and in you and in your seed all the families of the earth shall be blessed. Behold, I am with you and will keep you wherever you go, and will bring you back to this land; for I will not leave you until I have done what I have spoken to you." Then Jacob awoke from his sleep and said, "Surely the Lord is in this place, and I did not know it." And he was afraid and said, "How awesome is this place! This is none other than the house of God, and this is the gate of heaven!" Then Jacob rose early in the morning and took the stone that he had put at his head, set it up as a pillar, and poured oil on top of it. And he called the name of that place Bethel; but the name of that city had been Luz previously. Then Jacob made a vow, saying, "If God will be with me, and keep me in this way that I am going, and give me bread to eat and clothing to put on, so that I come back to my father's house in peace, then the Lord shall be my God. And this stone which I have set as a pillar shall be God's house, and of all that You give me I will surely give a tenth to You." Genesis 28:10-22. Scripture mentions that Abraham the grandfather of Jacob erected an altar at this area where Jacob stopped to spend the night and rested his head on a stone for a pillow. Jacob had an encounter with God that made a strong impression on him so he named the place 'Bethel' and worshipped there. Later in life, he was in trouble with the Hivites because Levi and Simeon massacred them on account of Shechem who had raped their sister Dinah. As a solution, God instructs Jacob to return to Bethel. "Then God said to Jacob, "Arise, go up to Bethel and dwell there; and make an altar there to God, who appeared to you when you fled from the face of Esau your brother." And Jacob said to his household and to all who were with him, "Put away the foreign gods that are among you, purify yourselves, and change your garments. Then let us arise and go up to Bethel; and I will make an altar there to God, who answered me in the day of my distress and has been with me in the way which I have gone." So they gave Jacob all the foreign gods which were in their hands, and the earrings which were in their ears; and Jacob hid them under the terebinth tree which was by Shechem. And they journeyed, and the terror of God was upon the cities that were all around them, and they did not pursue the sons of Jacob. So Jacob came to Luz (that is, Bethel), which is in the land of Canaan, he and all the people who were with him. And he built an altar there and called the place El Bethel, because there God appeared to him when he fled from the face of his brother. Genesis 35:1-7. Notice that on the way to Bethel, Jacob instructs his household to get rid of all their idols that was significant of sanctification. The consequence was that "And they journeyed, and the terror of God was upon the cities that were all around them, and they did not pursue the sons of Jacob." Awesome!!! Bethel is an encounter of the Holy Spirit anointing that unveils the essence of reverence. Irreverence is a plague that has infested the hearts of many believers today. It has its roots in Church history where there was an attempt to contemporize Christianity wherever possible. About a decade ago, it was a Friday, one week prior to easter and I was at home when the Holy Spirit whispered to me "you ought to have been in Church today." I was startled and begun to reflect on what I heard. I searched the scriptures and realized that it was the feast of Passover and Resurrection. My thoughts raised within me – 'why was is called 'Easter'?'. From historical records, I found out that Easter was the name of a pagan feast that was celebrated around the same time as Passover and Resurrection. To contemporize Christianity, the name of the pagan feast 'Easter' had now replaced 'Passover and Resurrection'. This divine encounter reshaped my attitude towards the 'Feasts of the Lord' which are the 'Appointed Times' for divine visitations. 'Moed' is the Hebrew for 'Appointed Times' and it is core to our fellowship with God. He visits the earth at these times whether we are diligent to reverence Him or not. "But you have come to Mount Zion and to the city of the living God, the heavenly Jerusalem, to an innumerable company of angels, to the general assembly and church of the firstborn who are registered in heaven, to God the Judge of all, to the spirits of just men made perfect, to Jesus the Mediator of the new covenant, and to the blood of sprinkling that speaks better things than that of Abel. See that you do not refuse Him who speaks. For if they did not escape who refused Him who spoke on earth, much more shall we not escape if we turn away from Him who speaks from heaven, whose voice then shook the earth; but now He has promised, saying, "Yet once more I shake not only the earth, but also heaven." Now this, "Yet once more," indicates the removal of those things that are being shaken, as of things that are made, that the things which cannot be shaken may remain. Therefore, since we are receiving a kingdom which cannot be shaken, let us have grace, by which we may serve God acceptably with reverence and godly fear. For our God is a consuming fire." Hebrews 12:22-29. Every divine visitation of the appointed times is for a very specific intention of God to quicken and furnish the anointing upon our lives. Like regular maintenance of a vehicle which is scheduled periodically by the recommendation of the manufacturer, the anointing upon our lives is renewed during the 'appointed times'. In the same way that a poorly maintained automobile is susceptible to breakdowns and a short shelf life, so is one who does not reverence the appointed times. Furthermore, reverence is an essential element of any process or method of work that indulges the anointing. Our encounter at Bethel gives us the ability to discern the reverence or irreverence of any formula, equation, process or method of work. Irreverence is godlessness and so it shows how antichrist a process of service or product is. Such a service or product that lacks reverence is also devoid of the anointing!

Jericho - This is the landmark and reference point encounter for warfare. Jericho is a method of the Holy Spirit anointing to rebuke and overcome opposition, resistance, conflict, and competition. Rebuke is a key word whenever there is a war that involves God's people. The word of God that circumcises us at Gilgal, and is the basis of our reverence at Bethel, is the basis of any rebuke of those who oppose us in a war. The victor of such a war is one who is gauged as more compliant with divine truth. Conquest of the Promised Land by the Israelites necessitated victory over the city of Jericho. This was a royal city where significant personalities of these heathen nations resided. It was the most formidable fortress built with very high walls of stone. They were confident that Israel will fail to breach its walls. "And it came to pass, when Joshua was by Jericho, that he lifted his eyes and looked, and behold, a Man stood opposite him with His sword drawn in His hand. And Joshua went to Him and said to Him, "Are You for us or for our adversaries?" So He said, "No, but as Commander of the army of the Lord I have now come." And Joshua fell on his face to the earth and worshiped, and said to Him, "What does my Lord say to His servant?" Then the Commander of the Lord's army said to Joshua, "Take your sandal off your foot, for the place where you stand is holy." And Joshua did so." Joshua 5:13-15. Prior to engaging the city of Jericho in warfare, Joshua has an encounter with the Commander of the army of the Lord. This is believed by some theologians to be the Lord Jesus Christ or at best an angel. To underscore the essence of rebuke as the determinant of who wins a war, when Joshua asks on whose side is the Commander of the Lord's army, He answers 'neither'. Victory is reserved for which army would be gauged as compliant with divine truth. Subsequently, Joshua is instructed to take off his shoes, after which he is given directions of how to engage the city of Jericho. "Now Jericho was securely shut up because of the children of Israel; none went out, and none came in. And the Lord said to Joshua: "See! I have given Jericho into your hand, its king, and the mighty men of valor. You shall march around the city, all you men of war; you shall go all around the city once. This you shall do six days. And seven priests shall bear seven trumpets of rams' horns before the ark. But the seventh day you shall march around the city seven times, and the priests shall blow the trumpets. It shall come to pass, when they make a long blast with the ram's horn, and when you hear the sound of the trumpet, that all the people shall shout with a great shout; then the wall of the city will fall down flat. And the people shall go up every man straight before him." Joshua 6:1-5. Priests blowing trumpets ahead of priests carrying the ark of the covenant would march around the city of Jericho. The walls of Jericho would fall on the seventh day after a long blast of the trumpet and a great shout. Victory over Jericho would be a supernatural feat. The ark of the covenant was symbolic of the judgments of God proclaimed by the priests blowing trumpets ahead of it. The walls of Jericho represented all that the heathen nations had devised to resist Israel. It included a practice of the inhabitants of Jericho where all their belongings were dedicated to their idol gods. This way, Jericho was not simply a physical fortress but also a demonic fortress. "Now the city shall be doomed by the Lord to destruction, it and all who are in it. Only Rahab the harlot shall live, she and all who are with her in the house, because she hid the messengers that we sent. And you, by all means abstain from the accursed things, lest you become accursed when you take of the accursed things, and make the camp of Israel a curse, and trouble it. But all the silver and gold, and vessels of bronze and iron, are consecrated to the Lord; they shall come into the treasury of the Lord." Joshua 6:17-19. The instruction for the Israelites not to take possession of the spoils of war from the city of Jericho was an indication that these items were devoted to demonic spirits. These items were charged tokens of demonic spirits and could invoke demonic interference among the Israelites. Though Jericho was defeated according to the Commander of the army of the Lord's instruction, the next battle against Ai was a disaster for Israel. An Israelite named Achan violated the instruction to abstain from the spoils of war at Jericho and hid these items among his stuff. Though Ai was a smaller community of people, Israel was unable to defeat them and the Lord revealed what Achan had done. Achan and his family and their possessions were destroyed, and Israel recovered divine favor to win wars in the Promised Land.

Jordan - This is the landmark and reference point encounter for supernatural manifestations. Jordan is a method of the Holy Spirit anointing that disrupts natural sequences to manifest the mercy of God. The divine covenant manifests God's mercy as a bridge to crossover for signs, wonders and miracles. As the Israelites approached the Promised Land from the wilderness, they conquered some territory west of the Jordan River though a greater part of the land promised was east of the Jordan. However, God explicitly commanded that all the men of Israel go across the Jordan to help secure the entire Promised Land. "So it was, when the people set out from their camp to cross over the Jordan, with the priests bearing the ark of the covenant before the people, and as those who bore the ark came to the Jordan, and the feet of the priests who bore the ark dipped in the edge of the water (for the Jordan overflows all its banks during the whole time of harvest), that the waters which came down from upstream stood still, and rose in a heap very far away at Adam, the city that is beside Zaretan. So the waters that went down into the Sea of the Arabah, the Salt Sea, failed, and were cut off; and the people crossed over opposite Jericho. Then the priests who bore the ark of the covenant of the Lord stood firm on dry ground in the midst of the Jordan; and all Israel crossed over on dry ground, until all the people had crossed completely over the Jordan." Joshua 3:14-17. Without boats, the Israelites crossed the Jordan by a supernatural feat of the Ark of the Covenant. God's mercy is a bridge by which we crossover from the natural to the supernatural. The Promised Land is the most significant change that we experience based on God's promises and our experiences at this space are predicated by the mercies of God. To exercise the fullness of the anointing upon Elijah, Elisha needed to capture the Jordan encounter. "Now Elijah took his mantle, rolled it up, and struck the water; and it was divided this way and that, so that the two of them crossed over on dry ground." 2 Kings 2:8. Here, Elijah's mantle like the Ark of the Covenant, orchestrated the bridge into the supernatural.

Chariots of Fire: Consistent manifestations of the supernatural works of God demonstrated through His servants are characterized as a 'move of God'. A move of God is predicated on synergy of the Spirit and spiritual mentoring. "Then it happened, as they continued on and talked, that suddenly a chariot of fire appeared with horses of fire, and separated the two of them; and Elijah went up by a whirlwind into heaven. And Elisha saw it, and he cried out, "My father, my father, the chariot of Israel and its horsemen!" So he saw him no more. And he took hold of his own clothes and tore them into two pieces. He also took up the mantle of Elijah that had fallen from him, and went back and stood by the bank of the Jordan. Then he took the mantle of Elijah that had fallen from him, and struck the water, and said, "Where is the Lord God of Elijah?" And when he also had struck the water, it was divided this way and that; and Elisha crossed over." 2 Kings 2:11-14. Elijah was involved in a 'move of God' that involved his confrontation of King Ahab's idolatrous reign and orchestrated a major revival in Israel. As his divinely appointed successor, Elisha needed to understand the dynamics of the 'move of God'. "And so it was, when they had crossed over, that Elijah said to Elisha, "Ask! What may I do for you, before I am taken away from you?" Elisha said, "Please let a double portion of your spirit be upon me." So he said, "You have asked a hard thing. Nevertheless, if you see me when I am taken from you, it shall be so for you; but if not, it shall not be so." 2 Kings 2:9-10. A divine encounter was key to a double portion of the anointing and Elisha experienced it as chariot of fire that appeared with horses of fire. Elisha's reaction: "My father, my father, the chariot of Israel and its horsemen!" unfolds the essence of the encounter that is synergy of the spirit and spiritual mentoring.

Synergy of the Spirit is the collaboration of God's servant with God and angels. Ezekiel's divine encounter sheds more light. "Now as I looked at the living creatures, behold, a wheel was on the earth beside each living creature with its four faces. The appearance of the wheels and their workings was like the color of beryl, and all four had the same likeness. The appearance of their workings was, as it were, a wheel in the middle of a wheel. When they moved, they went toward any one of four directions; they did not turn aside when they went. As for their rims, they were so high they were awesome; and their rims were full of eyes, all around the four of them. When the living creatures went, the wheels went beside them; and when the living creatures were lifted up from the earth, the wheels were lifted up. Wherever the spirit wanted to go, they went, because there the spirit went; and the wheels were lifted together with them, for the spirit of the living creatures was in the wheels.

Seed And Harvest In A Concurrent Era

When those went, these went; when those stood, these stood; and when those were lifted up from the earth, the wheels were lifted up together with them, for the spirit of the living creatures was in the wheels." Ezekiel 1:15-21. An easy way to describe the wheels of the Spirit is to think of a vehicle accessory known as a spinner wheel. It is an inner wheel ornament, which spins independently inside of a wheel itself when the vehicle is in motion and continues to spin even when the vehicle stops moving. The move of God never constitutes independent actions or programs of man, rather, it is always a collaboration with angels to manifest God's mercies wherever it is deserved.

Spiritual mentoring is another core of any move of God. Elisha's exclamation: "My father, my father, the chariot of Israel and its horsemen!" is significant here. Also known as discipleship, the model of spiritual mentoring is found throughout the scriptures and more significantly in the ministry of our Lord Jesus Christ. Another illustration of the move of God is to think of the various layers of an onion bulb that has several layers of onions within itself. Though the outer layer is dried or dead, the inner layers remain fresh and edible. The move of God often evolves in layers of manifestation through the model of discipleship. When there is no discipleship, the move of God grinds to a halt. Like a vehicle not operated and left in the cold of winter for a long period may require a jumpstart, so is the instance of the lack of spiritual discipleship. Elijah suffered a lot to jumpstart the move of God in his era and got so exhausted that he requested an early retirement. God granted this request because Elijah's predicament was legitimate. Elijah the prophet discipled Elisha who was a large-scale farmer to carry on with the move of God. Gehazi the servant of Elisha who could have inherited the prophet was overly concerned and distracted with their financial situation and ended up coveting the riches of Naaman. He missed the encounter of the Jordan and became a leper. Interestingly, it was King Joash who inherited Elisha. "Elisha had become sick with the illness of which he would die. Then Joash the king of Israel came down to him, and wept over his face, and said, "O my father, my father, the chariots of Israel and their horsemen!" 2 Kings 13:14. Here, the king of Israel is mentored by Elisha the prophet to carry on with the move of God.

Crossover Jordan: Elisha took over the mantle of Elijah at the Jordan encounter and returned towards Jericho by wielding this mantle over the Jordan. "Then he took the mantle of Elijah that had fallen from him, and struck the water, and said, "Where is the Lord God of Elijah?" And when he also had struck the water, it was divided this way and that; and Elisha crossed over." 2 Kings 2:14. This was the beginning of Elisha's phase of the move of God. Core to every move of God is the mission to manifest the mercies of God where it is deserved. Our Lord Jesus announced His mission at the onset of His ministry. "So He came to

Seed And Harvest In A Concurrent Era

Nazareth, where He had been brought up. And as His custom was, He went into the synagogue on the Sabbath day, and stood up to read. And He was handed the book of the prophet Isaiah. And when He had opened the book, He found the place where it was written: "The Spirit of the Lord is upon Me, because He has anointed Me to preach the gospel to the poor; He has sent Me to heal the brokenhearted, to proclaim liberty to the captives and recovery of sight to the blind, to set at liberty those who are oppressed; To proclaim the acceptable year of the Lord." Then He closed the book, and gave it back to the attendant and sat down. And the eyes of all who were in the synagogue were fixed on Him. And He began to say to them, "Today this Scripture is fulfilled in your hearing." Notice that the anointing unveils God's mercy for the poor, brokenhearted, captives, blind, oppressed etc. Injustice programed into natural sequences are disrupted by signs, wonders and miracles. Natural sequences of day and night; seedtime and harvest; cold and heat; winter and summer are all manifestations of the Chronos that was Noah's blessings we still enjoy today. The Chronos is why businesses and those involved in the occult can plan and leverage the predictability of the elements to foster their schemes. However the move of God interrupts the Chronos through the Kairos to manifest God's mercies to those who are deserving.

Seed And Harvest In A Concurrent Era

Day and night are the natural sequence for what happens within each twenty-four period. While day is synonymous with righteousness, night depicts unrighteousness. Wicked people, corporations and institutions that intend to oppress others use dark or hidden schemes. A move of God unravels such schemes: ""For behold, the day is coming, burning like an oven, and all the proud, yes, all who do wickedly will be stubble. And the day which is coming shall burn them up," says the Lord of hosts, "that will leave them neither root nor branch. But to you who fear My name the Sun of Righteousness shall arise with healing in His wings; And you shall go out and grow fat like stall-fed calves. You shall trample the wicked, for they shall be ashes under the soles of your feet on the day that I do this," says the Lord of hosts." Malachi 4:1-3. This prophetic promise indulges God's move to cause the day to manifest healing for those oppressed by the hidden schemes of the wicked. A spiritual day is not calculated as a twenty-four period rather, it a framework where the move of God is actively manifesting through God's servants. An instance is when a group of heathen nations in the Promised Land joined forces to fight against Israel. "And it happened, as they fled before Israel and were on the descent of Beth Horon, that the Lord cast down large hailstones from heaven on them as far as Azekah, and they died. There were more who died from the hailstones than the children of Israel killed with the sword. Then Joshua spoke to the Lord in the day when the Lord delivered up the Amorites before the children of

Israel, and he said in the sight of Israel: "Sun, stand still over Gibeon; and Moon, in the Valley of Aijalon." So the sun stood still, and the moon stopped, till the people had revenge upon their enemies. Is this not written in the Book of Jasher? So the sun stood still in the midst of heaven, and did not hasten to go down for about a whole day." Joshua 10:11-13. We see how twenty-four hours could be stretched beyond the limitations of the Chronos to foster fullness of the supernatural works of God. Days that are stretched to disrupt night cycles orchestrate miracles of regeneration. Another instance that is recorded in John 5:1-9: "After this there was a feast of the Jews, and Jesus went up to Jerusalem. Now there is in Jerusalem by the Sheep Gate a pool, which is called in Hebrew, Bethesda, having five porches. In these lay a great multitude of sick people, blind, lame, paralyzed, waiting for the moving of the water. For an angel went down at a certain time into the pool and stirred up the water; then whoever stepped in first, after the stirring of the water, was made well of whatever disease he had. Now a certain man was there who had an infirmity thirty-eight years. When Jesus saw him lying there, and knew that he already had been in that condition a long time, He said to him, "Do you want to be made well?" The sick man answered Him, "Sir, I have no man to put me into the pool when the water is stirred up; but while I am coming, another steps down before me." Jesus said to him, "Rise, take up your bed and walk." And immediately the man was made well, took up his bed, and walked. And that day was the

Seed And Harvest In A Concurrent Era

Sabbath." The angel that stirred up this water pool was evidence that points to miracles of regeneration. These are miracles that occur when we yield to the convictions of God's word. This man who got healed by Jesus was there for thirty-eight years and never had someone to place him in, when the angel stirred the water of the pool. Jesus shows up on the Sabbath day and instructs him: "Rise, take up your bed and walk." The man did as he was told and got healed instantly. Interestingly, there was an opposition that erupted as a result of this miracle. "The Jews therefore said to him who was cured, "It is the Sabbath; it is not lawful for you to carry your bed." He answered them, "He who made me well said to me, 'Take up your bed and walk.'" Then they asked him, "Who is the Man who said to you, 'Take up your bed and walk'?" But the one who was healed did not know who it was, for Jesus had withdrawn, a multitude being in that place. Afterward Jesus found him in the temple, and said to him, "See, you have been made well. Sin no more, lest a worse thing come upon you." The man departed and told the Jews that it was Jesus who had made him well. For this reason the Jews persecuted Jesus, and sought to kill Him, because He had done these things on the Sabbath. But Jesus answered them, "My Father has been working until now, and I have been working." Therefore the Jews sought all the more to kill Him, because He not only broke the Sabbath, but also said that God was His Father, making Himself equal with God. Then Jesus answered and said to them, "Most assuredly, I say to you, the Son can do nothing of Himself, but what He sees the Father do; for whatever He does, the Son also does in like manner." John 5:10-19. False doctrines propagated by religious leaders can impede the manifestation of miracles of regeneration. This is the reason that for every move of God, His servants must understand and function in the methods of the anointing. Divinely inspired preaching and teaching of God's word convicts people to take steps that foster the manifestation of miracles. God's word is the light of day that breaks patterns of night manifestations.

Seedtime and harvest are the natural sequence for what happens when we invest our life, time, and resources. Every kind of seed has its period of cultivation till harvest. While some seeds may generate a harvest within twenty-four hours, others may take five or more years. Assuming someone has been subject to oppression for several years, when their oppression ends, and they sow a seed of their divine purpose it may take several years for them to reap a harvest. ""Behold, the days are coming," says the Lord, "when the plowman shall overtake the reaper, and the treader of grapes him who sows seed; the mountains shall drip with sweet wine, and all the hills shall flow with it." Amos 9:13. This prophetic scripture indulges the supernatural wonders of redemption where there is a disruption of the natural sequence of the Chronos. The move of God would orchestrate overlapping of seed and harvest. Acts 9 records the instance of Paul's encounter with our Lord Jesus Christ on the road to Damascus where his mission was to persecute Christians. After the divine encounter he was totally transformed overnight and started preaching Christ everywhere. It was an instance of death and resurrection. There are certain instances where we may have been under human systemic or demonic bondage for several years and in a divine encounter, we receive an explicit instruction to die to a vice. Obedience to such an instruction triggers an instant resurrection so that we can begin to enjoy the long overdue fruits of harvest.

Cold and heat are the natural sequence for impacts of the atmosphere. While a cold atmosphere is significant of spiritual apostasy, heat unveils the signs of spiritual revival. "And it shall come to pass afterward that I will pour out My Spirit on all flesh; your sons and your daughters shall prophesy, your old men shall dream dreams, your young men shall see visions. And also on My menservants and on My maidservants I will pour out My Spirit in those days." Joel 2:28,29. This prophetic promise signaled manifestations of God's move for revival of His people. Peter the apostle invokes this promise as the premise for the manifestations that took place at the birth of the New Testament Church. "When the Day of Pentecost had fully come, they were all with one accord in one place. And suddenly there came a sound from heaven, as of a rushing mighty wind, and it filled the whole house where they were sitting. Then there appeared to them divided tongues, as of fire, and one sat upon each of them. And they were all filled with the Holy Spirit and began to speak with other tongues, as the Spirit gave them utterance." Acts 2:1-4. The signs that manifested on the day of Pentecost led to the salvation of three thousand souls. Without a shadow of doubt, it was obvious that God was moving through the disciples of Jesus to foster revival. After his resurrection, Jesus instructed the disciples: "And He said to them, "Go into all the world and preach the gospel to every creature. He who believes and is baptized will be saved; but he who does not believe will be condemned. And these signs will follow those who believe: In My name they will cast out demons; they will speak with new tongues; they will take up serpents; and if they drink anything deadly, it will by no means hurt them; they will lay hands on the sick, and they will recover." So then, after the Lord had spoken to them, He was received up into heaven, and sat down at the right hand of God. And they went out and preached everywhere, the Lord working with them and confirming the word through the accompanying signs." Mark 16:15-20. Preaching of the gospel ignites faith for the manifestation of supernatural signs. The day of Pentecost was just the beginning and the revival continued to spread to all places where the disciples went to preach the gospel.

Autumn, winter, spring, and summer are the natural sequence for the weather seasons. These weather seasons determine core human activities as well as failings. Joel the prophet proclaims that the move of God would be characterized by miracles of restoration. "And I will restore to you the years that the locust hath eaten, the cankerworm, and the caterpiller, and the palmerworm, my great army which I sent among you." Joel 2:25. Each of the four creatures mentioned represent the four stages of metamorphosis of the locust. It reveals human systems and demonic structures for disenfranchisement. "I will destroy the winter house along with the summer house; the houses of ivory shall perish, and the great houses shall have an end," says the Lord." Amos 3:15. In ancient times, kings had four kinds of palaces where they resided during the four weather seasons. They had prisons for holding those who offended during these seasons.

During autumn, kings resided in their farmhouses where their fields were cultivated with seed. Anyone who offended in relation to this activity was kept in an autumn prison. At winter, kings stayed at their winter palace that was designed to keep them warm. Anyone who offended in relation to the elements was held at the winter prison. An instance was when God revealed to Jeremiah their default of the Sabbaths and the consequence of captivity in Babylon. "Now it came to pass in the fourth year of Jehoiakim the son of Josiah, king of Judah, that this word came to Jeremiah from the Lord, saying: "Take a scroll of a book and write on it all the words that I have spoken to you against Israel, against Judah, and against all the nations, from the day I spoke to you, from the days of Josiah even to this day. It may be that the house of Judah will hear all the adversities which I purpose to bring upon them, that everyone may turn from his evil way, that I may forgive their iniquity and their sin."... "Now the king was sitting in the winter house in the ninth month, with a fire burning on the hearth before him. And it happened, when Jehudi had read three or four columns, that the king cut it with the scribe's knife and cast it into the fire that was on the hearth, until all the scroll was consumed in the fire that was on the hearth. Yet they were not afraid, nor did they tear their garments, the king nor any of his servants who heard all these words. Nevertheless Elnathan, Delaiah, and Gemariah implored the king not to burn the scroll; but he would not listen to them. And the king commanded Jerahmeel [e]the king's son, Seraiah the son of Azriel, and Shelemiah the son of Abdeel, to seize Baruch the scribe and Jeremiah the prophet, but the Lord hid them. Jeremiah 36:1-3,22-26. King Jehoikin was offended by the prophetic message Jeremiah gave about pending captivity of Israel by the Babylonian king. He burnt the scroll in the winter palace fireplace and sought to imprison Jeremiah but the Lord hid him.

Spring was the season for wars so kings lived in tents and camps. Those who offended as it pertained to warfare were held with shackles at the war camp. "Now about that time Herod the king stretched out his hand to harass some from the church. Then he killed James the brother of John with the sword. And because he saw that it pleased the Jews, he proceeded further to seize Peter also. Now it was during the Days of Unleavened Bread. So when he had arrested him, he put him in prison, and delivered him to four squads of soldiers to keep him, intending to bring him before the people after Passover. Peter was therefore kept in prison, but constant prayer was offered to God for him by the church. And when Herod was about to bring him out, that night Peter was sleeping, bound with two chains between two soldiers; and the guards before the door were [c]keeping the prison. Now behold, an angel of the Lord stood by him, and a light shone in the prison; and he struck Peter on the side and raised him up, saying, "Arise quickly!" And his chains fell off his hands. Then the angel said to him, "Gird yourself and tie on your sandals"; and so he did. And he said to him, "Put on your garment and follow me." So he went out and followed him, and did not know that what was done by the angel was real, but thought he was seeing a vision. When they were past the first and the second guard posts, they came to the iron gate that leads to the city, which opened to them of its own accord; and they went out and went down one street, and immediately the angel departed from him. And when Peter had come to himself, he said, "Now I know for certain that the Lord has sent His angel, and has delivered me from the hand of Herod and from all the expectation of the Jewish people." Acts 12:1-11. This is a spring instance where Herod preempts war against the Church and kills James. When he saw that it garnered popularity with the Jews, he made a political calculation to expand this war. He arrested and imprisoned Peter under a quaternion force. The Church reacted by engaging in spiritual warfare, so God dispatched an angel and miraculously Peter was delivered from prison. Not long after that, Herod was destroyed by an angel.

Summer was the season for harvest and so those who offended in relation to harvest were imprisoned at the king's summer palace. In the same way Joseph was released from prison, the Kairos move of God destroys any imprisonment system that may hold us.

Seed And Harvest In A Concurrent Era

Part II

Seed And Harvest In A Concurrent Era

CHAPTER FOUR

WORLDLY SYSTEMS

In Daniel's prophecy, four kingdoms symbolized by various animals will emerge that will dominate the world at various points in time. These four kingdoms were symbolized by various metals in a prophetic revelation given to King Nebuchadnezzar in Daniel chapter two.

- Lion – Gold – Babylonian Era
- Bear – Silver – Persian Era
- Leopard – Bronze – Greek Era
- Beast – Iron – Roman Era

History records the Babylonian, Persian, Greek and Roman eras are those kingdoms, which reigned as world powers until the time of Christ. In today's world, these four kingdoms are operating together as one fundamental system, by which the kingdom of darkness holds on to the wealth of the world. As we read earlier from the book of Daniel chapter seven, the prophetic structure by which the world's kingdoms or systems are designed to thrive, is an indication of how national, state and city economies, corporations, financial institutions, educational institutions have positioned themselves to be successful. The scripture refers to every geographical territory controlled by a government, economic system, corporate enterprise, educational institution, social order, financial institution, or any other formidable system as a kingdom.

These kingdoms are symbolic of the strongholds that God instructed the Israelites to permanently destroy in any territory he assigned to them. "When the LORD your God brings you into the land you are entering to possess and drives out before you many nations—the Hittites, Girgashites, Amorites, Canaanites, Perizzites, Hivites and Jebusites, seven nations larger and stronger than you— and when the LORD your God has delivered them over to you and you have defeated them, then you must destroy them totally. Make no treaty with them, and show them no mercy. Do not intermarry with them. Do not give your daughters to their sons or take their daughters for your sons, for they will turn your children away from following me to serve other gods, and the LORD's anger will burn against you and will quickly destroy you. This is what you are to do to them: Break down their altars, smash their sacred stones, cut down their Asherah poles and burn their idols in the fire" Deuteronomy 7:1-5 (NIV).

The stronghold of any kingdom was rooted in the demonic system put in place to invoke the protection of demons. They were made up Sacred Stones, Asherah Poles (High Things), Altars and Idols. Several years later after Israel had established itself in the Promised Land, it was obvious that they had not destroyed these demonic systems and as a result were constantly living in the shadow of aggression from their neighbors. God raised up Jeremiah as a prophet to tackle the fundamental reasons behind Israel's struggles. "Then the word of the LORD came to me, saying: "Before I formed you in the womb I knew you; Before you were born I sanctified you; I ordained you a prophet to the nations." Then said I: "Ah, Lord GOD! Behold, I cannot speak, for I am a youth." But the LORD said to me: "Do not say, 'I am a youth,' For you shall go to all to whom I send you, And whatever I command you, you shall speak. Do not be afraid of their faces, For I am with you to deliver you," says the LORD. Then the LORD put forth His hand and touched my mouth, and the LORD said to me: "Behold, I have put My words in your mouth. See, I have this day set you over the nations and over the kingdoms, To root out and to pull down, To destroy and to throw down, To build and to plant" Jeremiah 1:4-10. Notice the commission of

Seed And Harvest In A Concurrent Era

Jeremiah was twofold – To root out, pull down, destroy, and throw down constituted the first mandate to destroy the four parts of a demonic stronghold. The second mandate was to build and plant. It is important to note that you cannot build and plant kingdom institutions and structures without demolishing the demonic strongholds present. Just as the presence of demonic strongholds were the biggest impediment to Israel's economic and social stability, Christians today will not enjoy the fullness of the prosperity promised in the scriptures except the demonic structures of the world are spiritually destroyed.

The Apostle Paul places the demonic stronghold into a modern-day spiritual context. "For though we walk in the flesh, we do not war according to the flesh. For the weapons of our warfare are not carnal but mighty in God for pulling down strongholds, casting down arguments and every high thing that exalts itself against the knowledge of God, bringing every thought into captivity to the obedience of Christ, and being ready to punish all disobedience when your obedience is fulfilled" 2 Corinthians 10:3-6. Paul names the four aspects of a demonic stronghold – Arguments Against God's Word, High Things, Thoughts and Disobedience. Let us match these alongside Daniel's revelation and the revelation of strongholds to Moses and Jeremiah:

Seed And Harvest In A Concurrent Era

1. Lion – Gold – Babylonian Era – Sacred Stones – **Arguments Against God's Word**
2. Bear – Silver – Persian Era – Asherah Poles – **High Things (Ambitions)**
3. Leopard – Bronze – Greek Era – Altars – **Ungodly Thoughts**
4. Beast – Iron – Roman Era – Idols – **Disobedience**

The Apostle Paul says, "For the weapons of our warfare are not carnal but mighty in God for pulling down strongholds." This means that the scriptures furnish us with specific tools to overcome the four walls of any demonic system that may hinder our emotional, spiritual and financial fulfillment.

Seed And Harvest In A Concurrent Era

CHAPTER FIVE

WORLDLY RULES OR DIVINE PRINCIPLES

A constitution is drafted for a nation; a corporation establishes rules and regulations for its operations; a school establishes rules for teachers as well as students; an apartment complex makes rules for residents and financial institutions set rules for account holders and borrowers. Rules are the guidelines underlying the practices and conduct of people. They are the policies by which a local government sets standards for licensing professional practitioners, contractors as well as beneficiaries of opportunities. In Colossians 2:8-17, the Apostle Paul admonishes us: "Beware lest anyone cheat you through philosophy and empty deceit, according to the tradition of men, according to the basic principles of the world, and not according to Christ. For in Him dwells all the fullness of the Godhead bodily; and you are complete in Him, who is the head of all principality and power. In Him you were also circumcised with the circumcision made without hands, by putting off the body of the sins of the flesh, by the circumcision of Christ, buried with Him in baptism, in which you also were raised with Him through faith in the working of God, who raised Him from the dead. And you, being dead in your trespasses and the uncircumcision of your flesh, He has made alive together with Him, having forgiven you all trespasses, having wiped out the handwriting of requirements that was against us, which was contrary to us. And He has taken it out of the way, having nailed it to the cross. Having disarmed principalities and powers, He made a public spectacle of them, triumphing over them in it. So let no one judge you in food or in drink, or regarding a festival or a new moon or Sabbaths, which are a shadow of things to come, but the substance is of Christ". As Christians, we are warned to be careful about whatever the world refers to as 'principles'. Those who craft worldly rules usually shroud them with double standards. There are often hidden intentions that may not be immediately obvious. The consequence for breaking a rule in any system is often harsh and condemning. If you violate the constitution, you may end up in jail; if you break a corporate rule, you may lose your job as an employee; if you are late with your payments, you may be denied access to services; an apartment complex may evict you immediately; a financial institution may lower your credit rating or even recall loans you owe; and a school may suspend or dismiss you completely. Every system established by people who do not embrace Christ is likely to be undergirded with some rules that may be contrary to the principles of God's word. Such rules may not incorporate love and forgiveness, which are fundamentals of the scriptures.

Contrary to worldly rules that often promote Satan's agenda for society, the principles enshrined in the scriptures empower us to operate in God's love and forgiveness. They are designed to enable us to find the path to pursue purpose and destiny. "And you, being dead in your trespasses and the uncircumcision of your flesh, He has made alive together with Him, having forgiven you all trespasses, having wiped out the handwriting of requirements that was against us, which was contrary to us. And He has taken it out of the way, having nailed it to the cross. Having disarmed principalities and powers, He made a public spectacle of them, triumphing over them in it." God's word destroys the demonic obstacles that could prevent people from achieving their divine goals. This is why it must form the basis of every constitution, corporate rules, and institutional regulations. As Christians, we must never set rules and regulations in our establishments that do not allure to the fundamental objectives of God's word. We must promote and defend the values of love and forgiveness wherever we work. Upholding divine principles as the rationale behind our corporate rules is how we become competitive and ultimately overthrow worldly systems.

All scriptural principles are summarized into the ten basic principles of life commonly known as the 'Ten Commandments', which God gave to Moses on Mount Sinai. Today the Ten Commandments, which were previously displayed publicly in almost every institution in the United States to serve as a standard of the human conscience and judgment, have been barred by the government. People who do not want to be held to the standards of the scriptures have worked hard to alienate God's word from public display in society. The devil's agenda is to create a society that rejects righteousness as a standard of life.

Gold-Head

King Nebuchadnezzar's dream of an image with a gold head, silver chest, bronze thighs and iron mixed with clay legs was interpreted as the various kingdoms that will dominate the earth at some point. While Daniel revealed that King Nebuchadnezzar's Babylonian reign depicted the head of gold, the scriptures as well as history confirm the Persian reign as the silver chest, Greek reign as bronze thighs and the reign of the Romans as iron mixed with clay.

Seed And Harvest In A Concurrent Era

Of all the four metal components of Nebuchadnezzar's dream, gold is the most valuable followed by silver, bronze and iron consecutively. Interestingly, Daniel interprets that the kingdoms following Nebuchadnezzar's Babylonian reign will be inferior in the same consecutive fashion.

The Babylonians were known to have developed several laws based on the 'Code of Hammurabi' to establish a civil society and an outstandingly prosperous economic system. Similarly, by vigorously embracing the concept of the rule of law, the United States has evolved out of the doldrums of mediocrity and the ashes of civil war, to become the global superpower within two hundred years.

Gold has always been the original form of money accepted for transactions, a measure and standard of value. While the amount of gold one possesses is an indication of their level of riches, spiritually, wealth is also depicted by gold. Whoever controls gold becomes the center of gravity. In other words, if you can establish laws that directly affect money, you automatically become rich. If the king for instance wants to have some more money at their disposal, they simply increase the tax per head. A little change in rules could potentially make a company very rich or go bankrupt. To boost and protect their revenues, big corporations hire lobbyists to influence legislation in their favor. Personal rules like an individual who decides to be very frugal with resources, deny themselves of comfort and save a lot is a way to build riches. Wealth however is the spiritual dimension of gold and one can only amass this spiritual wealth by adopting the scriptural principles for financial success and prosperity. Money answers to the principles of any system designed to control it.

CHAPTER SIX

AMBITION OR DIVINE PURPOSES

A mbition is a strong determination to achieve great things. It is rare that you will find a normal person without the desire to accomplish something special as a lifetime achievement. Though some people have hideous ambitions to commit crime and other unimaginable feats, they also feel justified in their aspirations. There is really very little difference between someone who commits a crime by corporate greed and another who literally attacks someone at gunpoint to rob them. One of the primary roots of the world's economic decline is the pursuit of ambition, which is commonly known as the 'Pursuit of Happiness'.

Seed And Harvest In A Concurrent Era

The pursuit of ambition for anyone who has no relationship with Christ is to subject oneself to the Lust of the Flesh, Lust of the Eyes and the Pride of Life. It is an opening up of oneself to fulfill the devil's agenda for this earth. No wonder the devil often promotes those who yield themselves to pursue goals he inspires them to work at. In the pursuit of ambition, whatever ways and means you achieve your goal is not measured to any standard so long as the desired results are achieved. The scriptures tell of times in the history of Israel when society was characterized with so much crime because everyone was in pursuit of their own ambitions. Habakkuk the prophet was appalled and resolved to confront the challenge the right way. "I will stand my watch and set myself on the rampart, and watch to see what He will say to me, and what I will answer when I am corrected. Then the LORD answered me and said: "Write the vision and make it plain on tablets, That he may run who reads it. For the vision is yet for an appointed time; But at the end it will speak, and it will not lie. Though it tarries, wait for it; Because it will surely come, It will not tarry. "Behold the proud, His soul is not upright in him; But the just shall live by his faith. "Indeed, because he transgresses by wine, He is a proud man, And he does not stay at home. Because he enlarges his desire as hell, And he is like death, and cannot be satisfied, He gathers to himself all nations and heaps up for himself all peoples. "Will not all these take up a proverb against him, And a taunting riddle against him, and say, 'Woe to him who increases

What is not his—how long? And to him who loads himself with many pledges'? Will not your creditors rise up suddenly? Will they not awaken who oppress you? And you will become their booty. Because you have plundered many nations, All the remnant of the people shall plunder you, Because of men's blood and the violence of the land and the city, And of all who dwell in it. "Woe to him who covets evil gain for his house, That he may set his nest on high, That he may be delivered from the power of disaster! You give shameful counsel to your house, Cutting off many peoples, And sin against your soul. For the stone will cry out from the wall, And the beam from the timbers will answer it. "Woe to him who builds a town with bloodshed, Who establishes a city by iniquity! Behold, is it not of the LORD of hosts That the peoples labor to feed the fire, And nations weary themselves in vain? For the earth will be filled with the knowledge of the glory of the LORD, As the waters cover the sea" Habakkuk 2:1-14.

Habakkuk describes ambition as an insatiable desire that feeds on demonic intoxication to accumulate riches. This trait is so obvious with most rich people in today's world. Their assets are good collateral, so they accumulate several loans to fund any project and venture that seems feasible or lucrative. To keep some of these ventures profitable, they devise several schemes, which often rob employees of their due benefits, investors of their dividends and clients of their legitimate consideration. The 2009 world economic recession unveiled unimaginable corporate greed by famous financial institutions and collaborating entities. Some of these institutions designed flamboyant and complex investment securities with the aim of duping people and succeeded in robbing unsuspecting investors. Some of the culprits were arrested and their assets liquidated to reimburse their victims. It is not honorable to rob society with elaborate schemes to build your estate. In the absence of the desire to pursue divine purpose, perpetuating the vices of wickedness and greed are inevitable. Habakkuk decided to seek God's purpose for his life. Standing upon our watch is to align our lives with the principles of God's word. This is also known as righteousness, and it places us in the pathway of God's favor. To stand upon a rampart is to start seeking God through prayer. If we seek God through prayer, He comes through with answers. Especially when we seek God about His purpose for our lives, He will not be hesitant to reveal our purpose, which is the reason why we were created.

Divine purpose unveils our divine potentials in a unique way. It brings us to focus on accomplishing those things that impact society positively. The pursuit of purpose stimulates our relevance and creativity. We all become a blessing to our generation and not a hangover. The reason why population growth is a problem to most economies is that we have not encouraged the pursuit of purpose. There is no single human being that is supposed to be a problem to society if we can harness their divine potentials. The pursuit of ambition muzzles our creativity and makes us victims - an unnecessary addition to the problems of society.

Silver Chest and Arms

The Persian reign that followed the Babylonian reign was significant of silver chest and arms in the image of King Nebuchadnezzar's dream. Silver has always been of lesser value than gold. It is significant of human life. The silver cord is man's connection with life. Judas Iscariot sells Jesus Christ for thirty silver coins as well as many transactions for human life in the scriptures were conducted with silver.

King Cyrus is the Persian ruler that released the Jews from captivity. Well before King Cyrus is born, the prophet Isaiah prophesies about Cyrus in Isaiah chapter forty-five. God will raise Cyrus up, prosper him, elevate him, and burden him with the mission to set Israel free from captivity. Though Cyrus is not a worshipper of God Almighty, his life is designed with the purpose of fulfilling God's desire for Israel after seventy years in captivity. In line with this divine objective, Cyrus is filled with passion to accomplish what he sees as the right thing to do. Purpose is always driven by a passion from within us. If our passion is lustful then we hinge on the vices that could potentially destroy us ultimately. Genuine passion is the well spring of the Holy Spirit within us. "Jesus said, if you are thirsty come to me and drink, for out of your belly shall flow rivers of living water" John 7:37. Out of our belly, the springs of life flow inspirations from the divine Spirit of the living God. We cannot be conduits of the devil if we ignite the springs of living water that God has wired us with. Our real life is the life of God within us.

Across the world, people are saddled with poverty, debt, sickness, diseases, crime, social delusion, divorce and several vices. Many people today are facing extreme economic hardships just as much as governments and organizations that are at the brink of bankruptcy. Educated people cannot find jobs and those employed hardly have job security as they could be laid off at just any point in time. Unable to understand why, some have resolved there is no God and have become atheists. The question people ask is – "if the scriptures say that God the creator of the universe is love, kind, merciful and compassionate then why will He place us here on earth to experience all the pain, grief and heartaches of life?" It is immediately apparent that the reasons for these calamities on earth are either divine or human. If we should assume for a moment that these problems are divine, we will find it inconsistent with other created things that we as human beings crave and work hard or sometimes fight wars to secure. For instance, God created land and anyone who possesses land is wealthy. Land that is rich in nutrients is suitable for agriculture, and land without agricultural nutrients may become a housing development, factory site, quarry site or mined for precious minerals and other resources. The Saudis where aggressively looking for water in the desert when they discovered vast deposits of oil that is responsible for their phenomenal riches. Without a shadow of doubt, it is evident that God created land, which is our habitation with so many goodies. Therefore, it is impossible to claim that He made a mistake with us the human beings whom He created to inhabit the earth and possess this land.

Many people start out in life with all the ideals and standards for the pursuit of happiness. They get a good education probably a college or professional degree, secure a good job, marry, and start a family, purchase a vehicle and home, subscribe to all kinds of insurance protection and so on. This can be a reality for most people until just one piece of the puzzle gets out of place resulting in loss of employment. If you can find another job within six months, then you will probably bounce back and catch up with time. However, if you are unable to find another job within six months, it begins to put a strain on your mind, your marriage and family. For most relationships, romance is hardly a mutual pleasure in the absence of finance or if the family breaks down because of financial strain, then you are back to square one. Life becomes extremely stressful, and depression may set in.

Rejection of our divine purpose is the beginning of our dilemma and struggle in life. We cannot just pursue happiness and find sustainable happiness in the ideal job or career, ideal marriage partner, ideal home, or investment. No matter how well we check the facts surrounding our choices, there is no sound alternative to the pursuit of divine destiny. The pursuit of happiness is the false aspiration the devil offers us as citizens of his world. He is a thief and only tricks us into those investments that he can eventually rob from us when we get to the peak of his plan. Like a pyramid scheme, our world collapses before us without notice.

It is terrible to imagine that God who created all of us had no great purpose in mind other than to plunge us into this chaos of unfortunate hardships in just every aspect of human life. It is obviously our rejection of God's purpose for our lives that forms the basis of all unnecessary suffering and pain. Let us look at an extreme example in the scriptures with the story of Sodom and Gomorrah. Sodom and Gomorrah were twin cities where Lot the nephew of Abraham chose to reside. The people of Sodom and Gomorrah were so evil that God came down to affirm their deeds if it was indeed a reality. Abraham attempted to intercede for these people only to find out that there were less than ten righteous people in the twin cities, so God was justified to destroy them. Eventually God destroyed Sodom and Gomorrah but spared Lot and his two daughters. Today, though we are spared from destruction because there are enough people doing good to spare the earth from destruction, there are not enough righteous to sustain the balance of prosperity.

Most people who accept responsibility for their frustrations often ascribe it to deficiencies in their humanity. I am not as intelligent as I ought to be, not connected enough and so on. The decision to create man was to replicate the spiritual and intellectual properties of God Himself. He made us in His own image and likeness! NOT MORE, NOT LESS! The devil saw the potential of Adam and Eve who were in the image and likeness of God and got jealous. Adam and Eve were endowed with dominion and majesty to conquer and rule the earth. This would have ended the devil's reign over the earth, so he hatched up a scheme to thwart the agenda of God. He knew if he has no dominion over man, then he will become a slave to man, so he resorted to trickery. He got Adam and Eve to reject their God given identity. WHENEVER YOU LOSE YOUR IDENTITY, YOU AUTOMATICALLY LOSE YOUR AUTHORITY. This is reason the Apostle Paul considers all that he has attained in life as rubbish in the face of the revelation of Christ about himself. The revelation of Christ provides the believer with the true picture of who they ought to be in the light of divine purpose. The Apostle Paul says, "that I may know Him, and the power of His resurrection, the fellowship of His suffering, if I may be conformed to His death and attain His resurrection". A divine revelation of Christ gives us a mirror image of who we ought to be in the light of divine purpose. It challenges us to die to the sinful nature. This requires us to reject the image that the devil has sought to establish in us. The nature of sin that is self-gratifying and self-centered must die. The selfish ambitions that feed into our ego and pride must die. It is only then that we can see a new man arise by the power of the resurrection of Christ. The same Spirit that raised Christ from the dead comes in to quicken our mortal bodies. Resurrection power comes alive in us and what was sown corruptible is transformed into incorruptible, our weakness is turned into power, our shame is turned into glory and what was natural in us becomes spiritual.

We are Seed

Biologically a human being starts out as a sperm that fertilizes an egg in the womb of a woman. A pregnant woman is referred to as having taken seed. All through the scriptures, we see the offspring of human beings being referred to as seed. Whether scientifically, sociologically, or spiritually it is accepted that every human being starts out as a seed, just in the same way a plant is cultivated by sowing a seed. The reproductive power of a seed is never evident until it is sown into the soil. The harsh environment of the soil always causes the seed to die. The only reason that a seed will germinate, grow into a plant, and bear fruit is because of the presence of water. Jesus Christ referred to himself as a seed that must die so as to multiply. He accepted the mission of the cross and freely spoke about it several times to His disciples. Jesus Christ taught those who gathered around Him to carry their own cross to be His disciples. To be a good disciple, you had to be willing to die to the course of this world including family relationships that were in opposition to your divine purpose as well as your own ambitions and desires that were contrary to God's will. To die means that you must become insensitive to the conditions around you. You only respond to the water of God's word that has the power to raise you up as a resurrected seed.

In Matthew chapter thirteen, Jesus also referred to God's word as the seed that was sown into various types of soils yielding different results based on the conditions of these soils. If God's word is seed then it is only right to say that when He breathed into Adam the breath of life, He literally spoke purpose into that clay work he had molded out of the dust of the earth. God's spoken purpose for our lives is what makes us a seed. Jesus puts it this way, "...the flesh counts for nothing; for it is the Spirit that quickens... the words that I speak, they are Spirit and they are life." The molded clay was without life until God spoke purpose to it. This is the reason all through the scriptures we find God restoring original identity to those He intended to use for any significant mission. Abram's name which means 'exalted father' was changed to Abraham 'father of many nations'; Jacob's name which means 'deceiver' was changed to Israel 'a prince who prevailed with God and man' and several other examples recorded in the scriptures. John the Baptist and Jesus Christ were both assigned names by the angels who announced their birth. A name is the nature and the character of an object or person. A good name defines the original purpose of a thing or being.

Failure to acknowledge God's prophetic purpose for a seed is the beginning of identity crisis. That seed wrongly named will constantly be at war with itself. God's purpose and the false identity will establish a mismatch in the soul of the seed. The Apostle Paul describes this scenario when he says "For we know that the law is spiritual, but I am carnal, sold under sin. For what I am doing, I do not understand. For what I will to do, that I do not practice; but what I hate, that I do. If, then, I do what I will not to do, I agree with the law that it is good. But now, it is no longer I who do it, but sin that dwells in me. For I know that in me (that is, in my flesh) nothing good dwells; for to will is present with me, but how to perform what is good I do not find. For the good that I will to do, I do not do; but the evil I will not to do, that I practice. Now if I do what I will not to do, it is no longer I who do it, but sin that dwells in me" Romans 7:14-20.

Recently I was teaching on this subject and the Holy Spirit impressed upon my heart to tell the audience to fast to seek their original identity. The results were phenomenal as it enabled those present to discover supernatural things pertaining to their divine purpose. Fasting is self-denial and it opens us up to experience a divine encounter with God. Jacob wrestled with an angel all-night to discover his identity in the light of a constant cycle of evil circumstances. In view of his identity crisis and consequent struggles, Jabez prayed fervently until God answered him. Discovering 'WHO AM I' is the greatest quest to unlock the hidden potentials in anyone. It is the first key to true success in life and enduring prosperity. If you can imagine walking on a street and no one notices you, no acknowledgement, no compliment, and no greetings. When your life does not light up the world around you, it is as though you are a ghost. Without form, void and darkness was the state of the earth before God lighted it up with the declaration 'Let there be light'. Frustration, poverty and failure are the landmarks of a person without identity. You cannot be acknowledged or complimented if you have no unique identity. When you need a table, you go to the furniture store to buy it. If you need a television, you go to the electronics store to purchase it. If you do not have an identity no one seeks you, for there is no reason to need you and no designated place to find you! Though you exist physically, people will relate to you as though - YOU ARE A GHOST APPEARING AS A SHADOW! Notice how people flock around the so called 'stars' sometimes just to take a glimpse of them or even get their autograph or pose with them for a photograph or just a handshake simply because they have distinguished themselves in an area of life. These 'stars' as we often call them, have established for themselves an identity!

Failure to identify potentials around you is the beginning of poverty. During the Wild West gold rush, the miners found out that there was a substance that stuck to their shovels and slowed down their excavation in search of gold. One miner complained about the sticky substance that hindered their mining to a jeweler to whom he often sold his gold, and the jeweler asked him to bring some of that sticky substance on his next trip from the mining fields. When he brought the sticky substance, the jeweler offered him more money because this was a far more precious material than gold. This miner went back to the fields and focused more of his attention on the abundant precious material he had previously considered a hindrance. Most of us live next door to neighbors who have potentials that could compliment ours and release our potentials in a substantial way, but we sometimes hate these neighbors or simply do not care who they are and never want to have anything to do with them. Our failure to harness potential is the primary reason why poverty prevails in society.

3-Dimensional

Then God said, "Let Us make man in Our image, according to Our likeness; let them have dominion over the fish of the sea, over the birds of the air, and over the cattle, over all the earth and over every creeping thing that creeps on the earth." So God created man in His own image; in the image of God He created him; male and female He created them. Then God blessed them, and God said to them, "Be fruitful and multiply; fill the earth and subdue it; have dominion over the fish of the sea, over the birds of the air, and over every living thing that moves on the earth" Genesis 1:26-28. Firstly, the decision to make man was within the framework of a three-dimensional God in concert with Himself. God the Father, the Son and the Holy Ghost are three in one. This is why God instructed Adam to eat from only three of the trees in the Garden of Eden – the tree pleasant to the sight, the tree of life and the tree good for food. The tree pleasant to the sight speaks of our soul, emotional, family destiny. It is the prophetic dimension of our lives where we all have the potential to prosper sociologically by having great relationships with family and friends. The tree of life speaks to our spiritual destiny. It is the priestly dimension of our lives where we have a role in the temple. Everyone must graduate from warming the pews and fulfill their divine assignment in the house of God. The tree good for food speaks to our body or financial destiny. It is the kingly dimension of our lives. Everyone must identify and pursue the career, profession or enterprise that God has ordained to bring them financial fulfillment.

Every tree is the product of a seed sown. The three trees man was told to cultivate would originate from seeds. We must cultivate the seed pleasant to the sight, seed of life and seed good for food to enjoy the fruit of these trees. If a seed is a word spoken by God as we have already discussed, then we need a revelation of our seed pleasant to the sight, seed of life and seed good for food. We are three-dimensional beings, so we all crave prosperity in our soul, spirit and body. We all have three environments that we relate to: Sociologically to our family and friends; Spiritually to God and angels; and financially to colleagues at work, clients and customers. In all these three environments, we want to experience prosperity which is only possible if we sow the right seeds.

Secondly, God made us in His image and likeness. This speaks of His spiritual character and physical nature. Two scriptures allure to this fact. First of all 2 Peter 1:2-9 tells us "Grace and peace be multiplied to you in the knowledge of God and of Jesus our Lord, as His divine power has given to us all things that pertain to life and godliness, through the knowledge of Him who called us by glory and virtue, by which have been given to us exceedingly great and precious promises, that through these you may be partakers of the divine nature, having escaped the corruption that is in the world through lust. But also for this very reason, giving all diligence, add to your faith virtue, to virtue knowledge, to knowledge self-control, to self-control perseverance, to perseverance godliness, to godliness brotherly kindness, and to brotherly kindness love. For if these things are yours and abound, you will be neither barren nor unfruitful in the knowledge of our Lord Jesus Christ. For he who lacks these things is shortsighted, even to blindness, and has forgotten that he was cleansed from his old sins." The power to live a godly life is infused into us when we embrace divine purpose. This then becomes our allure to keep step with the Holy Spirit, as He guides us towards our divine destiny. Arriving at the place of fulfillment becomes inevitable through our diligent relationship with God.

Finally, we understand who God is by physically observing creation. In Romans 8:20 the scripture says, "For since the creation of the world His invisible attributes are clearly seen, being understood by the things that are made, even His eternal power and Godhead, so that they are without excuse." By observing the character of created beings like the lion, eagle, ox and Jesus Christ in scripture, we get a glimpse of how God operates. If we emulate the character of Christ especially, there is no reason why we will not experience victory in all areas of our life. God has given every one an identity that wins, succeeds and prospers. There is no fault in any one of us. It is only when we accept and operate in our three-dimensional potentials, as well as embrace our godly attributes, that we enjoy the blessing of fruitfulness, multiplication, and dominion!

While the greatest breakthrough is to accept your divine purpose, the next task is to get your world to identify and accept this light. "For now we see in a mirror, dimly, but then face to face. Now I know in part, but then I shall know

Seed And Harvest In A Concurrent Era

just as I also am known" 1 Corinthians 13:12. You must grow in your divine identity until everyone acknowledges you in this light. Educating yourself with knowledge about the vocation is the first key to growth. Your divine purpose is your career, and you must invest in schooling yourself until you attain professionalism. Let it be among your personal goals to read relevant industry information, trends and developments so that you are never ignorant in your profession. Attend industry seminars and develop a passion for research in that industry. Never place financial gratification at the core of your preferences when making a choice of employment opportunities. Always choose the job that places you in the industry of your divine purpose so that you can develop skill through experience and increase your professional value.

CHAPTER SEVEN

FACTS AND GODLY PLANS

A ccurate data is the cornerstone of acceptable economic forecasts that are fundamental to any enterprise endeavor and project. Social, industrial and consumer patterns can all be measured and analyzed in the light of historical data. By incorporating relevant facts and trends into a plan, you may convince a bank to lend you the money required for a project. Most often, an institutional investor will not be convinced to purchase equity without facts brewed from historical analysis.

Thanks to the sacrifice of Noah that ushered in the time era, that make facts a very relevant component for investment predictability. During the concurrent era, basing an investment proposition on only factual analysis will become very illusive. Feasibility Studies based on historical data alone will fail to provide the solid basis of any investment. You will have to be in the pathway of truth to know exactly when, how, and where to invest. Truth is God's perspective of any given endeavor. Truth is the basis of a sound strategy. Divine strategy is a mix of divine principles and purposes brought into the framework of God's perspective of a given mission.

We gain God's perspectives through fellowship at the appointed times – Sabbath, Passover, First-fruits, Pentecost, Trumpets, Atonement and Tabernacles. These seven feasts were appointed times when God visited Israel to reveal His perspective of the times and what Israel ought to do. In the New Testament Dispensation, these seven feasts are intricately woven into our weekly fellowship with God as well as specific programs that we observe in obedience to the leading of the Holy Spirit. You will have to develop a faithful relationship with God and submission to a genuine under-shepherd of Christ to stay in tune with God's truth. Divine strategy will ultimately become the key factor that determines which projects or ventures prosper in the concurrent era.

Bronze Thighs

The reign of the Greeks was depicted as bronze in the dream of Nebuchadnezzar. Bronze is an alloy made up primarily of copper and perhaps tin, zinc or other metal. It was of lesser value than silver and was used mostly in the manufacture of weapons of war. While the additional metal component of a bronze alloy is mined from low lands, copper which is the primary element is mined out of hills. Significantly, the Greeks built their reign on the foundations of the Babylonian and Persian eras. History informs us that Alexander the Great was a young and very skillful Greek warrior who conquered the known world of his day. Undergirded with philosophy and ambition, he was in a unique position to leverage facts for strategic conquests. Strategic planning is the bedrock of successful endeavors. What wins a war is not necessarily the size of an army or the level of weaponry or ammunition available. Always, it is the most strategic army that wins a war. The ability to discipline oneself to some rules, develop clear-cut goals and have a grasp of the facts surrounding an objective is the key to a good plan.

Strategic Positioning

If you are very observant, you will notice how many new shops in your neighborhood started out with bright signs and prospects but shut their doors after a very short while. The statistics is about only two out of every ten businesses remain after five years. In reality, many of the ventures out there are either copycats or lack strategy. By classifying some as copycats, I am referring to businesses that start out without an original divine conviction. Some people go along with the saying that 'you do not need to be creative... just look down the street and do something that is working for others'. That is a terrible philosophy, which the scriptures refer to as emulations. God did not create anyone to be a copycat and that is why He gives each of us a unique DNA. If there is someone accomplishing exactly what you have been made for, then you are not necessary. To be a copycat or lack a unique strategy for your pursuit is tantamount to failure. This is a core reason most enterprises fail. There are so many aspects of our human existence crying desperately for the creativity that makes an enterprise strategic. Most often, we do not aspire to be creative because we do not want to pay the price. Strategy involves deep thinking, brainstorming, research, analysis of data, testing repeatedly. That sounds like too much work just to arrive at a strategic initiative, yet essential and fundamental if we are to become consistently successful.

King Solomon who was the wealthiest man on earth during his reign wrote in Ecclesiastes 10:10, "If the ax is dull, and one does not sharpen the edge, then he must use more strength; but wisdom brings success." If you can imagine yourself attempting to cut down a tree with a blunt axe, then you can immediately figure out how frustrating it is to pursue a venture in the absence of strategy. Strategy is the wisdom that produces success. It eliminates struggle from an endeavor.

Seed And Harvest In A Concurrent Era

Habakkuk the prophet saw the dysfunction evident in society and decided to tackle it the right way. "I will stand my watch and set myself on the rampart. And watch to see what He will say to me, And what I will answer when I am rebuked. Then the LORD answered me and said: "Write the vision and make it plain on tablets, that he may run who reads it. For the vision is yet for an appointed time; But at the end it will speak, and it will not lie. Though it tarries, wait for it; Because it will surely come, It will not tarry" Habakkuk 1:1-3.

- Step 1 - The right approach to destiny is to start out doing what we are told by the scriptures in every area of our lives. Obedience to the scriptures is the essence of standing on our watch.

- Step 2 - When we obey God's word, He becomes attentive to our prayers. Prayer is our spiritual tower that enables us see the future through the eyes of God. God's answer to our prayer is revelation. Revelation is the only way we can resist the rebuke of the devil as we press on toward destiny.

- Step 3 - The third step in the process was to write the vision and make it plain upon tablets that he may run that reads it. In other words, God told Habakkuk to craft a strategic plan. Such a plan should clearly spell out your goals and how every human resource and physical asset will be deployed to accomplish them.

- Step 4 - Finally every goal must be designated for accomplishment within the framework of divine timing.

After the flood of Noah's day, one of the great men that emerged was Nimrod. He is described in the scriptures as a mighty hunter. Success usually gives you a voice in society so he naturally became an authority figure. The scripture says the beginning of his kingdom was Babel. This is where he organized the world of his day to build a city with a tower that reached heaven. Nimrod was opposed to the plan of God for the earth. To build this rebellious city he chose to use substitutes for the fundamentals for building a tower. Instead of stones, he used bricks and in place of mortar they used asphalt. He advanced his goals until God came down and confused the language of those builders so the project was stalled. In the concurrent era, every plan that opposes God's design for the earth will be stalled.

CHAPTER EIGHT

SENTIMENTS AND ALLIANCES

F ear is that state of emotion that allures to those things that inhibit and threaten our sense of prosperity and security. Many people panic each time the media reports negative financial news about downward spirals of the capital markets. Fund Managers increase or decrease their investments in certain areas because of sheer sentiment, which is simply the fear of what may happen with particular industries, entities, government decisions or communities. Fear is absolutely the wrong premise for any investment or corporate pursuit. Instead of being subject to the sentiment of fear, we must rather pursue those challenges which when solved makes the world a better place for all. Society is plagued with many problems that we all shy away from. Self-centeredness constantly drives us all away from societal challenges. When people get overly ambitious, it is deeply rooted in their fears. Some of their pursuits may be inspired directly by the fear of social problems or their apparent inadequacies. To overcome these insecurities, some people join cults or fraternities.

Nations categorized as advanced can only boast at best of thirty percent of societal problems solved, while emerging nations may boast of twenty percent, and third world countries less than ten percent. Our categorization as either advanced, emerging or least developed, allures to the extent to which we have tackled issues that confront us sociologically, environmentally, and economically. If you live in a so-called advanced nation today, you will agree with me that there is so much evidence of sociological, environmental, and economic issues that the term advanced does not qualify as status. People still eat from trashcans, many are homeless, many are walking about with ailments in their bodies, crime is the largest content of all news and so on. We may be advancing, but not advanced!

Israel was in a similar state in the days of Isaiah the Prophet. In those days, they called societal issues burdens. The prophets were inspired with the burdens of Israel, and in the book of Isaiah 22, we discover how God intended the Israelites to confront these issues.

"What ails you now, that you have all gone up to the housetops, You who are full of noise, A tumultuous city, a joyous city? Your slain men are not slain with the sword, Nor dead in battle. All your rulers have fled together; They are captured by the archers. All who are found in you are bound together; They have fled from afar. Therefore I said, "Look away from me, I will weep bitterly; Do not labor to comfort me Because of the plundering of the daughter of my people." For it is a day of trouble and treading down and perplexity by the Lord GOD of hosts. Breaking down the walls and of crying to the mountain. Elam bore the quiver With chariots of men and horsemen, And Kir uncovered the shield. It shall come to pass that your choicest valleys shall be full of chariots, and the horsemen shall set themselves in array at the gate. He removed the protection of Judah. You looked in that day to the armor of the House of the Forest; You also saw the damage to the city of David, That it was great; And you gathered together the waters of the lower pool. You numbered the houses of Jerusalem, And the houses you broke down to fortify the wall. You also made a reservoir between the two walls for the water of the old pool. But you did not look to its Maker, Nor did you have respect for Him who fashioned it long ago. And in that day the Lord GOD of hosts called for weeping and for mourning, For baldness and for girding with sackcloth. But instead, joy and gladness, Slaying oxen and killing sheep, eating meat and drinking wine: "Let us eat and drink, for tomorrow we die!" Then it was revealed in my hearing by the LORD of hosts, "Surely for this iniquity there will be no atonement for you, even to your death," says the Lord GOD of hosts. The Judgment on Shebna, Thus says the Lord GOD of hosts: "Go, proceed to this steward, To Shebna, who is over the house, and say: 'What have you here, and whom have you here, That you have hewn a sepulcher here, as he who hews himself a sepulcher on high, Who carves a tomb for himself in a rock? Indeed, the LORD will throw you away violently, O mighty man, and will surely seize you. He will surely turn violently and toss you like a ball into a large country; There you shall die, and there your glorious chariots shall be the shame of your master's house. So I will drive you out of your office, and from your position he will pull you down. 'Then it shall be in that day, that I will call My servant Eliakim the son of Hilkiah; I will clothe him with your robe And strengthen him with your belt; I will commit your responsibility into his hand. He shall be a father to the inhabitants of Jerusalem and to the house of Judah. The key of the house of David I will lay on his shoulder; So he shall open, and no one shall shut; And he shall shut, and no one shall open. I will fasten him as a peg in a secure place, and he will become a glorious throne to his father's house. 'They will hang on him all the glory of his father's house, the offspring and the posterity, all vessels of small quantity, from the cups to all the pitchers."

First, the Israelites were saddled with various sociological, environmental and economic issues just like any place on earth today. Everyone was thrown into survival mode. Life is so hard, I need to just get a job, pay my bills and get a life! It sounds like a familiar song you hear with many people especially in New York where I operate from. People often abandon their dreams and goals at the slightest confrontation with opposing circumstances. Most people have not developed the mindset of viewing opposition as part of the framework of circumstances that are designed to stir us in the right direction. The right approach is to go headlong and confront challenges with all the emotional, spiritual, and physical potentials we are divinely endowed with. Instead of being confrontational and advancing in the face of opposition, we often retreat and give up entirely on the pursuit of purpose. We enter survival mode and liquidate the elements of our divine destiny just to meet our needs and pay bills. Those confronted with family problems are quick to resort to divorce. Those who are not able to pay for further education abandon their career goals and seek a survival or mediocre job. Those who fail to get resources to advance their dream enterprise file for bankruptcy.

Seed And Harvest In A Concurrent Era

Secondly, instead of seeking God the Israelites abandoned him completely. They refused to fast and pray because they had found a way to get two or more jobs that enabled them to rent an apartment, pay their bills and probably have a little change for a vacation. It is also common to find most people today doing two to three jobs a day and yet saddled with so much debt and in constant financial distress. To abandon the dream is never the choice of those who ultimately win. Challenges must stir us toward God who is our maker! In 1 Corinthians 10:13 the scripture says: "No temptation has overtaken you except what is common to mankind. And God is faithful; he will not let you be tempted beyond what you can bear. But when you are tempted, he will also provide a way out so that you can endure it." There is always a divine strategy that we need to engage to overcome challenges that oppose our dreams and goals. God always provides the way out. Most often, people become so overwhelmed with the enormous size of the situation that they do not see how a divine intervention can help them out. Like David, we must always believe in a God who can work through five stones to defeat the sophisticatedly armed giant of a Goliath. Seeking God stirs us to look inward and upward. When we ask God for wisdom, He reveals our untapped potentials which when we engage, we find the resources to make progress. In addition, He reveals what principles we must engage to invoke angelic help. Angels only help and facilitate us at the point where our steps align with divine principles.

Finally, God mentions two people – Shebna and Eliakim. Sheba was the steward, governor or in today's context a Chief Executive Officer of an enterprise. The root of his failure is refusal to confront challenges headlong. Like the people of his day, he found a way to dodge taking responsibility for the issues, by liquidating the resources of divine destiny to build a temporary hedge of protection. This is the mindset of today's leaders and constituents alike that are directly responsible for our economic woes. For instance, when a corporation faces financial turbulence, they immediately lay off workers, which add to unemployment. Seldom do corporations review their human resource profiles to harness them for strategic redeployment in view of challenges. As a result of his failure to seek the wisdom to confront challenges, God decided to relieve Shebna of the position of leadership and reassign it to Eliakim. The mission Shebna failed to accomplish, the principles he failed to adopt was the reason why the royalty, the prosperity and legacy he could have attained was reassigned to Eliakim who was willing to take up the burden and tackle it God's way.

Iron and Clay Legs

The reign of the Romans was depicted as iron legs with feet of iron and clay. Iron is the least in value of the other metal components of Nebuchadnezzar's dream. Iron is used for making tools for work. The Romans built their reign on the foundation of the Babylonian, Persian and Greek eras. The

Seed And Harvest In A Concurrent Era

Romans were very organized militarily and had constructive goals for each domain they conquered. After conquering a region, they immediately built roads, barracks, aqueducts, coliseums and set up a system for governance. The Roman reign was the completion of the four walls of the worlds system. It was pursuit based on principles, purposes and planning. Within these four walls is where human emotional, spiritual, and financial aspirations are held. In other words, it is impossible to be fulfilled emotionally, spiritually, and financially without either submitting to the system or defeating the system. Iron is significant of the royals of the Roman era while the clay is significant of the peasants in the system. There are always double standards in the Roman system. One standard favors the royals at the expense of the peasants in the system. Today, the royals of the Roman system are not monarchs rather they are those in society who have become very successful at their endeavors. They band together as formal or informal fraternities to advance in their pursuits and consolidate themselves. The peasants of the Roman system are usually oblivious to the ways by which the royals operate to position themselves as exploiters.

Across the world today, Christians are praying for revival and so an awakening is imminent. We need healing from the leprosy, the scents, blindness, dumbness, deafness, doubt, and guilt that estranges us from God's glory.

Part III

Seed And Harvest In A Concurrent Era

CHAPTER NINE

THE LEPROSY FACTOR

I n Exodus chapter two, the story is recorded of how the Egyptians subjected Israel to slavery and the dramatic deliverance orchestrated by God through Moses. "Now there arose a new king over Egypt, who did not know Joseph. And he said to his people, "Look, the people of the children of Israel are more and mightier than we; come, let us deal shrewdly with them, lest they multiply, and it happen, in the event of war, that they also join our enemies and fight against us, and so go up out of the land." Therefore they set taskmasters over them to afflict them with their burdens. And they built for Pharaoh supply cities, Pithom and Raamses. But the more they afflicted them, the more they multiplied and grew. And they were in dread of the children of Israel. So the Egyptians made the children of Israel serve with rigor. And they made their lives bitter with hard bondage—in mortar, in brick, and in all manner of service in the field. All their service in which they made them serve was with rigor. Then the king of Egypt spoke to the Hebrew midwives, of whom the name of one was Shiphrah and the name of the other Puah; and he said, "When you do the duties of a midwife for the Hebrew women, and see them on the birthstools, if it is a son, then you shall kill him; but if it is a daughter, then she shall live." But the midwives feared God, and did not do as the king of Egypt commanded them, but saved the male children alive."

It is not uncommon in today's world to find governments who enact laws to subdue certain tribes or ethnic groups within a population. While the consequences of such legislation may be so obvious that it garners immediate public opposition, most of such laws may be so subtle that even the victims may not immediately understand the long-term effects. In the case of Israel, the Pharaoh of Egypt realized the population growth and economic prosperity trends were tilted in favor of the Israelites. Out of fear, the Pharaoh began to enact laws to diminish the prosperity and male population of the Israelites. During that period of Egyptian oppression, the Midwives were instructed by the decree of Pharaoh to kill any male born child of the Israelites. "And a man of the house of Levi went and took as wife a daughter of Levi. So the woman conceived and bore a son. And when she saw that he was a beautiful child, she hid him three months. But when she could no longer hide him, she took an ark of bulrushes for him, daubed it with asphalt and pitch, put the child in it, and laid it in the reeds by the river's bank. And his sister stood afar off, to know what would be done to him. Then the daughter of Pharaoh came down to bathe at the river. And her maidens walked along the riverside; and when she saw the ark among the reeds, she sent her maid to get it. And when she opened it, she saw the child, and behold, the baby wept. So she had compassion on him, and said, "This is one of the Hebrews' children." Then his sister said to Pharaoh's daughter, "Shall I go and call a nurse for you from the Hebrew women, that she may nurse the child for you?" And Pharaoh's daughter said to her, "Go." So the maiden went and called the child's mother. Then Pharaoh's daughter said to her, "Take this child away and nurse him for me, and I will give you your wages." So the woman took the child and nursed him. And the child grew, and she brought him to Pharaoh's daughter, and he became her son. So she called his name Moses, saying, "Because I drew him out of the water" Exodus 2:1-10.

Moses grew up in the palace of the Pharaoh and received the training set for the Egyptian princes. Because he was initially nursed by his biological parents, they let him know his true identity as an Israelite. "Now it came to pass in those days, when Moses was grown, that he went out to his brethren and looked at their burdens. And he saw an Egyptian beating a Hebrew, one of his brethren. So he looked this way and that way, and when he saw no one, he killed the Egyptian and hid him in the sand. And when he went out the second day, behold, two Hebrew men were fighting, and he said to the one who did the wrong, "Why are you striking your companion?" Then he said, "Who made you a prince and a judge over us? Do you intend to kill me as you killed the Egyptian?" So Moses feared and said, "Surely this thing is known!" When Pharaoh heard of this matter, he sought to kill Moses. But Moses fled from the face of Pharaoh and dwelt in the land of Midian; and he sat down by a well" Exodus 2:11-15. In exile, Moses married Zipporah the daughter of Jethro the Midianite priest. For forty years, Moses worked as a shepherd taking care of the sheep of Jethro his father-in-law. The Israelites back in Egypt were so frustrated with their oppression they began to organize themselves to seek God. "Now it happened in the process of time that the king of Egypt died. Then the children of Israel groaned because of the bondage, and they cried out; and their cry came up to God because of the bondage. So God heard their groaning, and God remembered His covenant with Abraham, with Isaac, and with Jacob. And God looked upon the children of Israel, and God acknowledged them" Exodus 2:23-25. God's solution for Israel's problem was Moses, who was in exile at this time. The parents of Moses saw him as a 'goodly child' when he was born. They had immediately recognized his potential as a seed of destiny and were willing to pay the price to preserve him for God's purpose. According to the decree of the Pharaoh, every Israelite male born child was to be thrown into the river so the parents of Moses decided to obey the king while trusting for God's intervention. A basket to preserve Moses was woven and it was placed in the river while his sister Miriam laid watch. This is how God orchestrated the deliverance of Moses and positioned him to be raised in Egypt's palace so he could understand how that leadership system worked. By all known standards, it is almost impossible to defeat a system you hardly understand. This is why Moses was best suited to confront the Pharaoh who was his playmate as a child and secure the deliverance of the Israelites.

"Now Moses was tending the flock of Jethro his father-in-law, the priest of Midian. And he led the flock to the back of the desert, and came to Horeb, the mountain of God. And the Angel of the LORD appeared to him in a flame of fire from the midst of a bush. So he looked, and behold, the bush was burning with fire, but the bush was not consumed. Then Moses said, "I will now turn aside and see this great sight, why the bush does not burn." So when the LORD saw that he turned aside to look, God called to him from the midst of the bush and said, "Moses, Moses!" And he said, "Here I am." Then He said, "Do not draw near this place. Take your sandals off your feet, for the place where you stand is holy ground." Moreover He said, "I am the God of your father—the God of Abraham, the God of Isaac, and the God of Jacob." And Moses hid his face, for he was afraid to look upon God. And the LORD said: "I have surely seen the oppression of My people who are in Egypt, and have heard their cry because of their taskmasters, for I know their sorrows. So I have come down to deliver them out of the hand of the Egyptians, and to bring them up from that land to a good and large land, to a land flowing with milk and honey, to the place of the Canaanites and the Hittites and the Amorites and the Perizzites and the Hivites and the Jebusites. Now therefore, behold, the cry of the children of Israel has come to Me, and I have also seen the oppression with which the Egyptians oppress them. Come now, therefore, and I will send you to Pharaoh that you may bring My people, the children of Israel, out of Egypt" Exodus 3:1-10. Moses was in exile because of his earlier attempts to broker peace between two Israelites who were in contention with one another. Previously he had killed an Egyptian who was oppressing an Israelite and these Israelites whom he attempted to advice rebuked his leadership intentions. You can imagine the sense of rejection Moses felt when his efforts were unappreciated by his fellow Israelites and the consequence being his present state of exile. He had attempted to lead God's people and failed. After forty years in exile, God shows up in a burning bush scenario to assign him with the mission of leading Israel out of Egyptian slavery. When Moses saw the strange phenomenon of the burning bush which was not consumed, he turned to move towards it. "So when the LORD saw that he turned aside to look, God called to him from the midst of the bush and said, "Moses, Moses!" And he said, "Here I am." Then He said, "Do not draw near this place. Take your sandals off your feet, for the place where you stand is holy ground" Why did God request Moses to take off his shoes? Our shoes are a barrier between us and the earth from which our body was formed. Shoes break our contact with the earth. All across the world, we find various natural resources embedded within the earth. In some places we find gold in abundance while in other places we may find crude oil, bauxite, or rich pasture and so on. Wherever any natural resource appears in abundance has always determined the prominent vocation or industry of those who reside there. If they identify and harness these natural resources, it becomes their immediate source of wealth and prosperity. Shoes alienate us from the potentials of the earth and spiritually the consequence is leprosy. Spiritually, leprosy is to break contact with God in your body. For this reason, lepers were not permitted to come near God's temple. When Moses argued with God about the mission to deliver the Israelites out Egypt, God revealed to him the spiritual state of his body. "Furthermore, the LORD said to him, "Now put your hand in your bosom." And he put his hand in his bosom, and when he took it out, behold, his hand was leprous, like snow. And He said, "Put your hand in your bosom again." So he put his hand in his bosom again, and drew it out of his bosom, and behold, it was restored like his other flesh" Exodus 4:6-7. Leprosy is the spiritual state of anyone who has no contact with God in relation to their divine assignment. Our hands and feet represent our works and ways. What we do and where we are render clues to whether we are spiritual lepers or not.

Brazen Laver

The first object of worship in the tabernacle of Moses was the brazen laver. It was a bowl that held water for washing the hands and feet of worshippers. The brazen laver was made of highly polished brass that gave a mirror reflection of those standing before it. Worshippers will wash until they were cleansed of dirt that could render them unclean. Significantly this process indicates how the word of God changes us to conform to God's works and ways. "...just as Christ also loved the church and gave Himself for her, that He might sanctify and cleanse her with the washing of water by the word, that He might present her to Himself a glorious church, not having spot or wrinkle or any such thing, but that she should be holy and without blemish" Ephesians 5:25-27. The principles enshrined in the scriptures are the standards by which we can mirror the works and ways of God. In our pursuit of purpose, we need to know how God accomplished creation. We must develop skills that mirror God's way of work. Contemporary education and apprenticeship will help us attain a certain degree of skill sets but then the ultimate craftsmanship that brings out the fullness of our creativity is vested with God. "For though by this time you ought to be teachers, you need someone to teach you again the first principles of the oracles of God; and you have come to need milk and not solid food. For everyone who partakes only of milk is unskilled in the word of righteousness, for he is a babe. But solid food belongs to those who are mature, that is, those who by reason of use have their senses exercised to discern both good and evil" Hebrews 5:12-14. Studying the word of God positions us to align our works with His. Engaging divine principles in accomplishing our assignment is how we demonstrate supernatural skills and manifest divine craftsmanship in our works. Always remember that just as with Adam during creation, God has called us to work with him in partnership to 'dress and keep' our garden. When we perform an assignment, people must immediately see it as the manifested handwork of God. The glory of God must manifest in whatever we do. With your body you have a relationship with the earth. The earth is the source of our wealth. We all have wealth in the earth depending on where God carved us out as individuals. So long as there is a disconnection between you and the God who created the earth, you cannot tap into the fullness of your wealth. By teaching Moses how to pursue his mission, God removed the leprosy factor that prevented Moses from having light in his body.

Iqwx lwlrq

Instruction from the scriptures shapes the human conscience to foster our intuitiveness. We are born with an empty conscience and whatever we observe or learn in society as good or bad works to either degenerate or develop our conscience. A bad conscience is where good values are considered bad and evil vices considered as good. Imagine a water filter where one deliberately fills with dirty water. The filter would quickly wear out being overburdened with dirt. Similarly, when we allow corrupt vices to fill our minds, our conscience cannot continue being pure. A good and pure conscience is where we study God's word as the determinant of our value system that translates into our intuitive capabilities.

CHAPTER
TEN

THE SMELL FACTOR

I n Medical Science, inability to smell odors with the nose is referred to as 'Anosmia'. Though God gave Moses the mandate to get the Israelites free from Egypt, the Pharaoh did not yield to nine out of the ten plagues invoked by Moses upon the Egyptians. Pharaoh's advisors reasoned with him saying "...don't you see Egypt is destroyed, let them go..." but the Pharaoh would not consent to that thought. His mindset was that the Israelites were free labor, and they could build more cities and make Egypt greater. God assured Moses that with the tenth and final plague, Pharaoh will let Israel go. By this plague God would change Israel's scent. Everyone has a scent. Dogs often smell and retain the scent of people to distinguish them. Your odor reflects the kind of grace that is upon your life. Grace comes from the Greek word 'Charis'. It is the perfume of God. In 2 Corinthians 2:14-17 the scripture says, "Now thanks be to God who always leads us in triumph in Christ, and through us diffuses the fragrance of His knowledge in every place. For we are to God the fragrance of Christ among those who are being saved and among those who are perishing. To the one we are the aroma of death leading to death, and to the other the aroma of life leading to life. And who is sufficient for these things? For we are not, as so many, peddling the word of God; but as of sincerity, but as from God, we speak in the sight of God in Christ." As believers in Christ, there is a fragrance that oozes out of our lives. Through our witness of Christ, we release into the atmosphere the odor of a spiritual perfume. This odor smells differently to two groups of entities. To God, His angels, and other believers we are a good scent. However, we are a bad smell to the devil, his demons and unbelievers.

Altar of Sacrifice

This altar was where animal sacrifices were offered to God. When Moses showed up to Pharaoh, the Pharaoh could not discern him. He had known Moses as an ordinary person because they grew up together in the palace. He could not discern that Moses was now a different person. Nine times Moses showed up before Pharaoh and there was no distinctive smell. The sacrifice of the Passover lamb was going to be the way to diffuse the smell of grace. Every

Seed And Harvest In A Concurrent Era

Israelite family was to offer up the sacrifice of the Passover Lamb, eat of it, burn the fat, and smear the blood on the doorposts of their homes. That night God sent an angel to execute the firstborn of every family that had not observed the Passover. The destruction angel distinguished families by the sign of the blood on their door posts and spared the Israelite families who had offered the Passover sacrifice. The Egyptian households who had not observed the Passover sacrifices were not spared and their firstborns were killed by the destruction angel. Pharaoh's firstborn child who would have succeeded the throne of Egypt was also among those executed by the destruction angel. Finally, the Pharaoh smelt the stench of Moses and Israel! The scent of the sacrifice of the Passover Lamb offered with fire had permeated the atmosphere. The Pharaoh was disgusted with it and the adverse effect of God's judgment upon his firstborn son. He quickly summoned Moses and Israel to get out of Egypt immediately. The Egyptians willingly gave up their gold, silver, and precious garments to the Israelites. Wealth transfer took place in favor of Israel. The moment you begin to smell foul to the kingdom of darkness, they will hurry you up to get out of hell and give up whatever was stolen from you.

The odor from their sacrifice was what distinguished the favor on Cain and Abel. Cain had the opportunity to give God an excellent sacrifice. To understand Cain's sacrifice, we must pay attention to Abel's sacrifice. "And in the

Seed And Harvest In A Concurrent Era

process of time it came to pass that Cain brought an offering of the fruit of the ground to the LORD. Abel also brought of the firstborn of his flock and of their fat. And the LORD respected Abel and his offering, but He did not respect Cain and his offering. And Cain was very angry, and his countenance fell. So the LORD said to Cain, "Why are you angry? And why has your countenance fallen? If you do well, will you not be accepted? And if you do not do well, sin lies at the door. And its desire is for you, but you should rule over it" Genesis 4:3-7. God always sets a standard for His requests from man. If Abel knew the standard, then Cain who was older should have known better. The sacrifice of Abel met the three standards of an excellent sacrifice which are Firstling, Flock and Fat. Cain's sacrifice was not accepted because it did not meet these standards of an acceptable sacrifice. He got angry but God still reached out to him. God encouraged Cain to get it right to smell good. We always have the chance to get it right. Most often people who are not willing to pay the price to get the right results become envious of those who prosper, resorting to undermining and character assassination.

Firstling

An acceptable sacrifice must qualify as firstling. In the bequeathing of inheritance, the firstborn was usually the heir. The firstborn will split the inheritance among their siblings equally but retain a double portion. With royal families, the firstborn was also the heir of the throne. This is the reason a sacrifice to God must always meet the standard of firstling. It must invoke a royal inheritance which was also a double portion. God only relates to people within the context of royalty. Every blessing from heaven allures to that reality. To qualify for blessing from His Majesty, it is essential that we step up to that dimension of royalty. The inheritance that God wants to give believers is royal because salvation through Jesus Christ automatically changes our status to 'noble seeds'. "He has not observed iniquity in Jacob, Nor has He seen wickedness in Israel. The LORD his God is with him, And the shout of a King is among them" Numbers 23:21. There is a shout of a king inside of us. God relates to the king inside of us.

When Gideon was threshing wheat in a winepress to hide it from the Midianite oppressors, the angel who was sent from God addressed Gideon as a 'mighty man of valor'. God never speaks to our state of mediocrity but rather to our potential for greatness. We are all potentially victorious royal seeds. The blessing of inheritance that comes from a sacrifice to God must meet the standards of royalty.

The crown of a king is the acknowledgement of royalty. We are all born into this world with hair on our heads. Hair is our natural crown that is significant of our burden of royalty. Traditionally, kings have domains or territories over which they reign. Similarly, as believers, we are assigned a domain or sphere of influence which becomes our natural burden or divine assignment. At a time in the history of Israel, they were oppressed by the Philistines, God sent an angel to Manoah and his wife. This Israelite couple was barren, and God sent an angel to inform them that they will conceive a child who will eventually deliver Israel from Philistine oppression. "...For behold, you shall conceive and bear a son. And no razor shall come upon his head, for the child shall be a Nazirite to God from the womb; and he shall begin to deliver Israel out of the hand of the Philistines" Judges 13:5. This child would be an answer to a major problem Israel was experiencing at the time. Samson was a generational seed to tackle a generational crisis. The cardinal instruction that will make this possible was that "no razor shall come upon his head". Significantly, it meant that Samson would have to bear the burden of Israel's deliverance all his life. The ability to function as a deliverer was tied to his responsibility to mitigate Israel's crisis. So long as his hair was unshaved, it was an indication that the burden was intact. Samson was able to defeat the Philistines in all the confrontations with them until his hair was shaved by Delilah. At this juncture he became powerless, was captured by the Philistines, kept in prison, and oppressed until his hair grew again. Once his hair grew, the anointing upon his life was restored and with one feat, he defeated all the Philistine rulers of his time.

A royal sacrifice speaks to the burden for which God released you to this earth. If you bear the burden of your assignment, you fulfill the chief requirement of an acceptable sacrifice. Jesus puts it this way, "...If anyone desires to come after Me, let him deny himself, and take up his cross, and follow Me" Matthew 16:24. Like Jesus, offering up His life as a sacrifice for the redemption of mankind, everyone has a cross to carry. To bear this cross, it is essential that we shed off our worldly aspirations and ambitions. The cross is significant of the unique divine responsibility to which we are individually assigned. Fulfilling your divine assignment gives you the first component of your smell.

No divine assignment is pleasant in any way. From the words of His prayer in the Garden of Gethsemane we realize that even Jesus had a difficulty with his cross. "Then Jesus came with them to a place called Gethsemane, and said to the disciples, "Sit here while I go and pray over there." And He took with Him Peter and the two sons of Zebedee, and He began to be sorrowful and deeply distressed. Then He said to them, "My soul is exceedingly sorrowful, even to death. Stay here and watch with Me." He went a little farther and fell on His face, and prayed, saying, "O My Father, if it is possible, let this cup pass from Me; nevertheless, not as I will, but as You will" Matthew 26:36-39. Ultimately, the sacrifice of Christ was accepted by God because he fulfilled the burden of the cross. "Therefore I will divide Him a portion with the great, And He shall divide the spoil with the strong, Because He poured out His soul unto death, And He was numbered with the transgressors, And He bore the sin of many, And made intercession for the transgressors" Isaiah 53:12. The way to take dominion over a kingdom always entails a fight. When we take up our cross, it is the fight for our domain, and the victory earns us the crown of royalty.

In the Old Testament Dispensation, animal sacrifices were accepted in substitution for the real sacrifice until Christ was offered on the cross. No amount of animal sacrifice can give off the actual scent of your royalty. This is why Jesus Christ puts the whole concept of sacrifice into perspective by teaching and demonstration of the sacrifice at the cross. Essentially, we are the sacrifice, and our smell of royalty is released through the work of fulfilling our divine assignment.

Flock

Another quality that qualified Abel's sacrifice as acceptable was that it was an animal. This is the essence of the blood requirement and to be able to feel pain. We might argue that Cain's sacrifice may have met the previous requirement of firstling since he brought fruits of the ground that represented his purpose but then it never had any blood element. Blood is essential because it is the atonement component of a sacrifice. "For the life of a creature is in the blood, and I have given it to you to make atonement for yourselves on the altar; it is the blood that makes atonement for one's life" Leviticus 17:11. Atonement simply means at-one-ment with God. Sin is the barrier that alienates us from God. However, it is blood that removes the barrier of sin. In the Old Testament era, the blood of animals were accepted as a temporary covering for sin. "For the law, having a shadow of the good things to come, and not the very image of the things, can never with these same sacrifices, which they offer continually year by year, make those who approach perfect. For then would they not have ceased to be offered? For the worshipers, once purified, would have had no more consciousness of sins. But in those sacrifices there is a reminder of sins every year. For it is not possible that the blood of bulls and goats could take away sins" Hebrew 10:1-4. However, in the New Testament era, Jesus Christ demonstrates through the cross, that permanent cleansing from sin begins with the offering of Himself as our eternal blood sacrifice. "For if the blood of bulls and goats and the ashes of a heifer, sprinkling the unclean, sanctifies for the purifying of the flesh, how much more shall the blood of Christ, who through the eternal Spirit offered Himself without spot to God, cleanse your conscience from dead works to serve the living God?" Hebrews 9:13, 14. To become the flock sacrifice, Jesus Christ offered himself first through the eternal Spirit and secondly without spot. Overall, this means that Jesus Christ became the perfect lamb by yielding to the leading of the Holy Spirit that kept Him from every action or way that could have corrupted him. "Therefore, when He came into the world, He said: "Sacrifice and offering You did not desire, But a body You have prepared for Me. In burnt offerings and sacrifices for sin You had no pleasure. Then I said, 'Behold, I have come—in the volume of the book it is written of Me—To do Your will, O God" Hebrews 10:5-7. In this era we are operating by the standards of a New Covenant that we subscribe to by accepting the blood sacrifice of Christ as our atonement from sin. The dynamics of this atonement is "the volume of the book that is written of me". Divine revelations leads each believer into their consecration.

Consecration means to be dedicated to God by sacrifice. It is only the eternal Spirit who can reveal these scriptures that are uniquely designed to bring each believer into their consecration with God. These scriptures come with specific instructions as to what we must avoid either by way of eating, actions, or manner of life. Remember, scripture lists a set of unclean animals that the Israelites were forbidden to eat. "Now the Lord spoke to Moses and Aaron, saying to them, "Speak to the children of Israel, saying, 'These are the animals which you may eat among all the animals that are on the earth: Among the animals, whatever divides the hoof, having cloven hooves and chewing the cud—that you may eat. Nevertheless, these you shall not eat among those that chew the cud or those that have cloven hooves: the camel, because it chews the cud but does not have cloven hooves, is unclean to you" Leviticus 11:1-4. In view of the

Seed And Harvest In A Concurrent Era

New Testament vision to the Apostle Peter of all animals now cleansed, today, this principle is a revelation of the dynamics of consecration. "...Peter went up on the housetop to pray, about the sixth hour. Then he became very hungry and wanted to eat; but while they made ready, he fell into a trance and saw heaven opened and an object like a great sheet bound at the four corners, descending to him and let down to the earth. In it were all kinds of four-footed animals of the earth, wild beasts, creeping things, and birds of the air. And a voice came to him, "Rise, Peter; kill and eat." But Peter said, "Not so, Lord! For I have never eaten anything common or unclean." And a voice spoke to him again the second time, "What God has cleansed you must not call common." This was done three times. And the object was taken up into heaven again" Acts 10:9-16. As a basic rule we understand that the Old Testament Dispensation is a shadow of the New Testament Dispensation. This means that most of the principles of the Old Testament Dispensations allure to some realities that can only be unveiled by divine revelation. Animal blood sacrifice was one of such principles and now by the vision given to the Apostle Peter we see that all unclean foods are now supernaturally cleansed and re-categorized as clean. The question is: Does that nullify the principle of clean and unclean animals? ABSOLUTELY NOT! Rather the dynamics of keeping ourselves without spot allures to a specific revelation by the Holy Spirit to each believer. Every believer has a unique consecration. Whatever we are convicted to abstain from by the leading of the Holy Spirit is how we keep ourselves from spot or blemish. When we fail to walk in this leading - this is the real sin. THE KEY TO CONSECRATION IS ABSTINENCE BY REVELATION. This is the essence of true fasting, which is self-denial of those things that the eternal Spirit points to us to specifically abstain from.

Remember when Noah came out of the ark after the flood, he offered up clean animals as sacrifice and God was pleased with him. "Then Noah built an altar to the Lord, and took of every clean animal and of every clean bird, and offered burnt offerings on the altar. And the Lord smelled a soothing aroma. Then the Lord said in His heart, "I will never again curse the ground for man's sake, although the imagination of man's heart is evil from his youth; nor will I again destroy every living thing as I have done" Genesis 8:20, 21. The aroma from clean animals offered invoked the covenant of preservation from destructive curses. Curses invoke demonic activity upon people. The curse upon Adam triggered so much demonic activity on the earth that God had to wipe out all living creature and start afresh with Noah's family and the animals preserved in the ark. With the offering of the blood of clean animals on the altar, Noah's sacrifice invoked the covenant of divine protection from curses.

The blood of Jesus Christ plays a cardinal role in our consecration. The blood of Jesus Christ is the hedge that protects us from the encroachment of devils that intend to harm or rob us of good. When we receive the leading of the Holy Spirit – do not say it, do not touch it, do not wear that dress, do not eat that food, do not drink that and so on: 'THIS IS THE VOICE OF THE BLOOD OF JESUS'! Abstinence by revelation is how we answer to the voice of the blood of Jesus Christ. That is how we are protected by the hedge of the blood of Jesus Christ.

One of the instructions of the angel to Manoah and his wife concerning Samson was that he should not touch unclean things. It was part of the requirements of the Nazirite vow. The Nazarite vow was a special consecration that any Israelite could observe to invoke unusual grace from God. Notable in the scriptures of those who invoked such grace were Samuel the prophet, who anointed Saul and David to become kings. John the Baptist invoked unusual grace as the forerunner and baptizer of Jesus Christ. By observing the Nazarite vow Samson consecrated himself to God and was used supernaturally to bring Israel out of Philistine oppression. By not touching or eating unclean things, a supernatural hedge was built around Samson. The Philistines tried countless times to trap him and hurt him to no avail. Samson was supernaturally protected by the hedge of his Nazarite consecration. The Israelites were protected from the destruction angel who executed the firstborn of all families in Egypt but did not enter the homes of the Israelites. The Israelites had obeyed God's instruction to observe the Passover sacrifice of a lamb and marked their doorposts with the blood. The destruction angel did not kill the firstborn of every Israelite family. Abstinence by revelation is how God protects us from the work of devils. This is how the blood of Jesus marks your doorpost. Every time you abstain by revelation, that is genuine fasting and what it does is, it demarcates your life and prevents the demons of hell from having a field day in your life and destiny. When you are convicted to abstain from having or doing something, God is not trying to prevent you from enjoying life, he does not want you to step into enemy territory. Whenever you have a strong negative conviction or feeling about something you about to do, it is most likely the voice of the blood speaking to you. That is the work of the blood in your life, revealing where there is a demarcation of your borders. The revelation of abstinence is the voice of the blood of Jesus building a hedge to our east, west, south, north, behind us, in front of us, on top of us and beneath us. We will not stumble because of revelation of abstinence.

Finally, the revelation of abstinence is unique to an individual and never a basis for a doctrine. It may become the basis of a generational consecration for one's offspring and nothing more. This means that your family may observe that abstinence if they are so convicted but not compulsorily so. No matter how much benefit a revelation of abstinence brings you as an individual, it is important that you do not teach others to observe it or demonize those who do not observe it.

Fat

An acceptable sacrifice is one that oozes abundant aroma. Abel's sacrifice met this standard to qualify as excellent. In the market where animals were sold, the fat looking animals were of higher value than the lean ones. God required the Israelites to always burn off the fat of their animal sacrifices, while the lean meat could be consumed. Fat always belonged to God, so to offer it up with fire was evidence of thanksgiving. The level of thanksgiving and appreciation of God's goodness was determined by the amount of fat released by fire into heaven. Noah built an altar when he came out of the ark in appreciation of how God had preserved his family from the flood. His motive was simply to acknowledge God's goodness. The sacrifice of Noah met the standard of a fat offering and so it invoked the blessing of prosperity for all mankind. "While the earth remains, Seedtime and harvest, Cold and heat, Winter and summer, And day and night Shall not cease" Genesis 8:27. Noah's sacrifice invoked the blessing of opposite cycles that orchestrate prosperity and increase. These cycles are fundamental to the equilibrium of the ecosystem. We can understand weather patterns and plan our work accordingly. When King Solomon offered a thousand animals in sacrifice to God, he invoked a divine visitation. When God said to him; 'ask whatever you desire', it meant that he was given a blank check. King Solomon asked for knowledge, a discerning heart and wisdom to reign over Israel. It was a good request by the standards of God, but then it was an overpayment for what he requested so God blessed King Solomon with riches in addition.

It takes great inspiration to offer up abundant sacrifices to God. Most often our selfish nature is more comfortable with hoarding our resources rather than giving. The question is 'how do I know that my offering qualifies as fat' since we do not offer animal sacrifices today. The Apostle Paul taught the Corinthian Church how to give fat sacrifices. "But this I say: He who sows sparingly will also reap sparingly, and he who sows bountifully will also reap bountifully. So let each one give as he purposes in his heart, not grudgingly or of necessity; for God loves a cheerful giver. And God is able to make all grace abound toward you, that you, always having all sufficiency in all things, may have an abundance for every good work. As it is written: "He has dispersed abroad, He has given to the poor; His righteousness endures forever." Now may He who supplies seed to the sower, and bread for food, supply and multiply the seed you have sown and increase the fruits of your righteousness, while you are enriched in everything for all liberality, which causes thanksgiving through us to God" 1 Corinthians 9:6-11. A fat sacrifice is always the product of genuine appreciation coupled with deep conviction. Paul says "so let each one give as he purposes in his heart, not grudgingly or of necessity". Though the mind is where we make intelligent decisions, spiritual decisions can only be made by searching the heart. The heart is the temple of God where we receive the conviction of purpose. The Holy Spirit is our source of conviction to know how much offering measures up to fat.

One of the conditions of the Nazarite consecration was abstinence from strong drink or wine. Alcoholic wine intoxicates and when consumed to a certain degree may influence people to do things they will not do normally. In the same way, the Holy Spirit may intoxicate us with inspiration to the degree that we fellowship with Him. The angel sent to inform Manoah's family of Samson's birth instructed that Samson had to abstain from strong wine. In other words, he was to remain constantly under the influence of the Holy Spirit. Today there are several ways we derive our inspiration and influence other than from the Holy Spirit. We are influenced by talk shows, worldly music, fictional books, and movies which may project values contrary to the godly standards expected of us. In some cases, believers have shied away from deep commitments to the kingdom as a direct result of the mockery and scorn of the world for certain aspects of spirituality, especially giving to advance the gospel. The inspiration of the Holy Spirit is the divinely ordained vehicle for driving our passion to glorify God to the acceptable level. There is a level of worship that throws the windows of heaven open for superabundant prosperity to flow down to the believer. Fat offerings are like abundant seeds a farmer cultivates. The level of seed sown determines the level of harvest yield.

Anosmia

When you have remained in an environment of bad odor for a long period of time, you become indifferent to the odor. Inability to smell with the nose is spiritually significant of being unable to discern. When you do not offer God acceptable sacrifices due to Him, you develop anosmia. Also, when we expect people to appreciate us instead of giving the thanksgiving to God for whatever good we do for them, we develop anosmia.

When Isaac was very old, he asked Esau to bring him venison so he could impart the blessing of posterity. Isaac was ignoring the fact that Esau had sold his birthright to his younger brother Jacob. Isaac wanted a sacrifice for himself which defies the principle of offering it up to God. As a result, he was unable to discern Jacob who had quickly prepared the venison at the suggestion of his mother in order to get his due blessing. "And Jacob went near unto Isaac his father; and he felt him, and said, The voice is Jacob's voice, but the hands are the hands of Esau. And he discerned him not, because his hands were hairy, as his brother Esau's hands: so he blessed him" Genesis 27:22-23.

Your sacrifice to God gives you a good scent that becomes a standard by which you discern others. One of the ways we make progress in life is by exchanging things of lesser value for those of greater value. Hence, we should desire the grace to be able to discern people, things, and atmospheres through offering up acceptable sacrifices to God. Without spiritual discernment, we end up exchanging things of higher value for those of lower value. Choosing friends, partners, job options, opportunities, procuring a house or property, jewelry, and making investments all require sound discernment otherwise we trade in the good for the bad. Your sacrifice invokes the grace to discern atmospheres and things charged with disfavor so that you can move away and gravitate towards atmospheres and things charged with divine favor.

Seed And Harvest In A Concurrent Era

CHAPTER ELEVEN

THE BLIND FACTOR

While Moses was in exile at Midian, living and working with his father in law, there was an inner frustration in the heart of Moses which drove him to lead the sheep to the backside of the desert. The cry in his heart brings him to the mountain of God where he saw a supernatural sight. The bush was on fire, but it was not burnt so he turned aside to look at the strange phenomenon. This was the first recorded instance where Moses ever saw a supernatural manifestation. Suddenly, his spiritual blindness was out of the way, and he was encountering a revelation of God's presence here on earth.

Seed And Harvest In A Concurrent Era

All around us are supernatural manifestations which we may not observe because of our spiritual blindness. Though the atmosphere in any true worship service is regarded as Mount Zion, the Holy Jerusalem with an innumerable company of angels and God Almighty present, with our natural eyes we cannot perceive them. In the book of Acts of the Apostles, the scripture records that while staying with Simon the Tanner in Joppa, the Apostle Peter fell into a trance in which he saw a vision of various animals descending from heaven. It was an interactive vision where he communicated back and forth with God. The scriptures also record in the Old Testament of an instance where the king of Syria sent soldiers to capture Elisha the prophet because Elisha always revealed his strategic plans to the king of Israel. When the Syrian army surrounded Elisha, his servant feared the Syrian army and so Elisha asked God to open the eyes of the servant. The servant was enabled to see the supernatural realm, with a great host of angels in position to defend Elisha from the Syrian army. Spiritual blindness can pose a great hindrance to deploying our potentials for prosperity. The Holy Place of the tabernacle of Moses was all covered up with curtain so that no external light came in. It was significant of the spiritual realm, which cannot be accessed by physical light. The seven branched lampstand also known as the candlestick was the only source of light in the Holy Place. The bible says our spirit is the candle of the Lord. "The spirit of man is the candle of the LORD, searching all the inward parts of the belly"

Seed And Harvest In A Concurrent Era

Proverbs 20:27. With your spirit you can see what is taking place in the spiritual realm. Those in the occult try to see into the spiritual realm illegally. They consult devils to rearrange circumstance to their advantage. This is witchcraft and there is a standing judgment for every witch, occultist and those who consult them. So how do we get to see into the realm of the spiritual? It is by building a relationship with God and understanding that the lampstand is our spirit. The fuel for the light of the lamp is oil. Oil comes from a seed that is broken, crushed, and pressed. From the things that are created, God gives us an opportunity to know him. When your life is broken, crushed, and pressed, oil is released. That oil is known as the anointing of the Holy Spirit. Zechariah the prophet received this understanding about the anointing. "Now the angel who talked with me came back and wakened me, as a man who is wakened out of his sleep. And he said to me, "What do you see?" So I said, "I am looking, and there is a lamp stand of solid gold with a bowl on top of it, and on the stand seven lamps with seven pipes to the seven lamps. Two olive trees are by it, one at the right of the bowl and the other at its left." So I answered and spoke to the angel who talked with me, saying, "What are these, my lord?" Then the angel who talked with me answered and said to me, "Do you not know what these are?" And I said, "No, my lord." So he answered and said to me: "This is the word of the LORD to Zerubbabel: 'Not by might nor by power, but by My Spirit,' Says the LORD of hosts. 'Who are you, O great mountain?

Seed And Harvest In A Concurrent Era

Before Zerubbabel you shall become a plain! And he shall bring forth the capstone With shouts of "Grace, grace to it!" Moreover the word of the LORD came to me, saying: "The hands of Zerubbabel have laid the foundation of this temple; His hands shall also finish it. Then you will know that the LORD of hosts has sent me to you. For who has despised the day of small things? For these seven rejoice to see the plumb line in the hand of Zerubbabel. They are the eyes of the LORD, which scan to and fro throughout the whole earth." Then I answered and said to him, "What are these two olive trees—at the right of the lamp stand and at its left?" And I further answered and said to him, "What are these two olive branches that drip into the receptacles of the two gold pipes from which the golden oil drains?" Then he answered me and said, "Do you not know what these are?" And I said, "No, my lord." So he said, "These are the two anointed ones, who stand beside the Lord of the whole earth" Zechariah 4. The Israelites had returned to Jerusalem from the Babylonian captivity and were in the process of rebuilding the temple. An angel revealed to Zechariah the spiritual framework by which this goal will be accomplished. The angel tells Zechariah that this huge project from God to the Governor Zerubbabel will not be accomplished by might or power. It will require the anointing of the Holy Spirit flowing through leadership with a supernatural vision.

Seed And Harvest In A Concurrent Era

Our mission on this earth is always huge in scope. Usually, a vision from God will be bigger than all our connections and resources. The first dynamic of the spirit is to recognize that we are a lamp. If there is no oil then the lights will be out. Oil must keep flowing in for the light to burn. The sources of the oil are the two trees beside the lamp. Secondly, the angel asks, "who has despised the day of small things?" In spite of how enormous a divine assignment may look like; it takes little resources and unassuming strategies of the Spirit to accomplish. 'Who are you, O great mountain? Before Zerubbabel you shall become a plain!' That mountain that stands before you is the difficulty of your assignment, the seemingly impossible obstacles that stand in the way. When Zechariah asked the angel about the significance of the seven branched lamp stand, the angel explained they are the seven spirits of God or the eyes of God in every part of the earth. God is omnipresent and sees everything taking place here on earth at every given point in time. He knows where you can find resources for the project at hand as well as all the support to make the vision a reality. In 1 Corinthians 2:9-12 the Apostle Paul says, "But as it is written: "Eye has not seen, nor ear heard, Nor have entered into the heart of man the things which God has prepared for those who love Him." But God has revealed them to us through His Spirit. For the Spirit searches all things, yes, the deep things of God. For what man knows the things of a man except the spirit of the man which is in him? Even so no one knows the things of God except the

Spirit of God. Now we have received, not the spirit of the world, but the Spirit who is from God, that we might know the things that have been freely given to us by God." With the natural eyes alone we may be blind to the things that God has made available to us. Every mission from God has automatic allocation of financial and material provision. The raw materials, resources, and support that we need to accomplish our assignment are already stashed up somewhere. The Holy Spirit reveals to us what is freely given to us for our pursuit of purpose.

Two instances of divine providence by revelation are recorded in the New Testament. First in Matthew 21:1-6, when Jesus was about to make entrance into Jerusalem, he sent two of his disciples to go to the village ahead where they will find a donkey and its colt tied to a tree. They should loosen them and if they are questioned, should respond that he had need of them. It happened exactly as Jesus had told the disciples and he rode majestically into Jerusalem. A second instance is recorded in Luke 22:7-13, "Then came the Day of Unleavened Bread, when the Passover must be killed. And He sent Peter and John, saying, "Go and prepare the Passover for us, that we may eat." So they said to Him, "Where do You want us to prepare?" And He said to them, "Behold, when you have entered the city, a man will meet you carrying a pitcher of water; follow him into the house which he enters. Then you shall say to the master of the house, 'The Teacher says to you, "Where is the guest room where I may eat the Passover with My disciples?"' Then he will show you a large, furnished upper room; there make ready." So they went and found it just as He had said to them, and they prepared the Passover. In all these instances Jesus Christ demonstrated that for every divine mission there is divine providence, however it takes a perfect sense of supernatural revelation to know where these resources are.

The Seven Eyes of the Spirit

In Isaiah 11:1-10 we get an understanding into the functioning of the seven spirits of God. "There shall come forth a Rod from the stem of Jesse, and a Branch shall grow out of his roots. The **Spirit of the LORD** shall rest upon Him, the Spirit of **wisdom** and **understanding,** the Spirit of **counsel** and **might,** the Spirit of **knowledge** and of the **fear of the LORD.** His delight is in the fear of the LORD, And He shall not judge by the sight of His eyes, nor decide by the hearing of His ears; But with righteousness He shall judge the poor, and decide with equity for the meek of the earth; He shall strike the earth with the rod of His mouth, and with the breath of His lips He shall slay the wicked. Righteousness shall be the belt of His loins, and faithfulness the belt of His waist. "The wolf also shall dwell with the lamb, the leopard shall lie down with the young goat, the calf and the young lion and the fatling together; and a little child shall lead them. The cow and the bear shall graze; their young ones shall lie down together; and the lion shall eat straw like the ox. The nursing child shall play by the cobra's hole, and the weaned child shall put his hand in the viper's den. They shall not hurt nor destroy in all My holy mountain, for the earth shall be full of the knowledge of the LORD as the waters cover the sea."

The seven spirits of God mentioned in this scripture are the seven eyes of God by which any godly leader can advance forward in the pursuit of a divine mission.

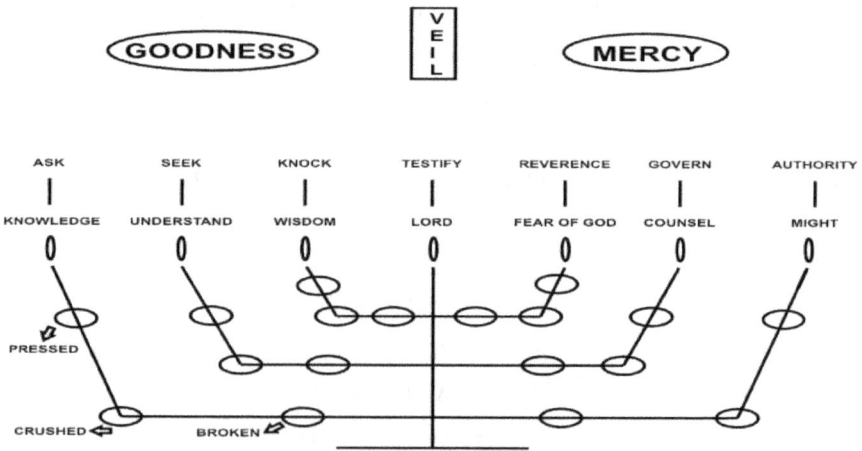

FIRST EYE - SPIRIT OF KNOWLEDGE

We ask for revelation knowledge through prayer. Most often we are frustrated with God for not answering our prayers. This is because we pray like little children asking their parents for a toy or candy. As adults we must realize that God prefers us to ask for knowledge to catch fishes instead of giving us fish all the time. The first eye of our spirit is to always ask God in prayer for knowledge of how to meet our needs, solve problems or tackle projects.

SECOND EYE – SPIRIT OF UNDERSTANDING

We seek for understanding by receiving the instruction of teaching. Usually, revelation knowledge which comes as an answer to prayer will require decoding. Teaching from the pulpit is designed to bring us insight to revelation knowledge. For instance, if you have prayed for knowledge and God gives you a dream with symbols, He does not expect you to go about looking for dream books to analyze your dream. Rather He expects you to seek understanding by requiring Him to bring clarity to your dreams through the teaching of His word. It is important that we attend Church services to position ourselves to understand God's word. The second eye is to pay attention to teaching from our spiritual leaders and draw the relationship with revelation knowledge we have received from God.

THIRD EYE – SPIRIT OF WISDOM

We knock for wisdom by applying revelation to our works. Wisdom is the practical aspect of revelation. It is the application of our understanding of divine principles to our works and ways. Not applying our insights of how to accomplish goals to our pursuits is counterproductive in our spiritual walk with God. We would be like trees that bear many leaves but fail to bear fruit. The Spirit of Wisdom is unleashed to us through micro-revelations that guide us in the pursuit of purpose. Such micro-revelation comes to us from the Holy Spirit nudging us concerning what to say or not to say, where to turn or avoid, which tool to use for a specific purpose and so on. The third eye is to apply divine principles and revelation in the administration of our pursuits.

FOURTH EYE – SPIRIT OF THE LORD

We overcome adversity by referencing the testimonies of God. The moment we start to apply divine principles and revelation in our pursuits, the kingdom of darkness takes notice that we are attempting an escape from their schemes so they likely will launch an attack. The kingdom of darkness throws barriers and obstacles that manifest as trials and temptations in the way of those who dare to apply divine revelation in their pursuits. To overcome such trials and temptations, we ought to call to memory the victories that God has secured for us in the past. First, we ought to encourage ourselves with such testimonies as well as look up similar instances in the scriptures where God orchestrated victory for His people. When Israel was confronted with the threats of Goliath, all the Israelite soldiers present except David were afraid and intimidated by his threats. "But David said to Saul, "Your servant used to keep his father's sheep, and when a lion or a bear came and took a lamb out of the flock, I went out after it and struck it, and delivered the lamb from its mouth; and when it arose against me, I caught it by its beard, and struck and killed it. Your servant has killed both lion and bear; and this uncircumcised Philistine will be like one of them, seeing he has defied the armies of the living God." Moreover David said, "The LORD, who delivered me from the paw of the lion and from the paw of the bear, He will deliver me from the hand of this Philistine" 1 Samuel 17:34-37. Secondly, we ought to declare these victories during warfare with the enemy. We overcome the kingdom of darkness by the words of our testimony. During his contest with Goliath, David declared the testimonial of the God of Israel to invoke divine intervention. "Then David said to the Philistine, "You come to me with a sword, with a spear, and with a javelin. But I come to you in the name of the LORD of hosts, the God of the armies of Israel, whom you have defied. This day the LORD will deliver you into my hand, and I will strike you and take your head from you. And this day I will give the carcasses of the camp of the Philistines to the birds of the air and the wild beasts of the earth, that all the earth may know that there is a God in Israel. Then all this assembly shall know that the LORD does not save with sword and spear; for the battle is the LORD's, and He will give you into our hands" 1 Samuel 17:45-47. The fourth eye is to reference how God defeated a similar enemy in the past for self-motivation as well as a declaration in warfare against our enemies.

FIFTH EYE – SPIRIT OF THE FEAR OF THE LORD
We demonstrate reverence for God by honoring Him with our lives as worship. "Therefore, I urge you, brothers and sisters, in view of God's mercy, to offer your bodies as a living sacrifice, holy and pleasing to God—this is your true and proper worship." Romans 12:1. If we acknowledge that God is our source of providence and preservation, then we must be faithful to whatever tasks He has assigned us. Often, people resign from their divine assignments because they may be going through certain difficulties. Regardless of how the enemy works against our tranquility, it should not become an excuse for not fulfilling our divine assignments. Keep on sacrificing yourself to fulfil your divine assignment which translates into odors of spiritual worship.

SIXTH EYE – SPIRIT OF COUNSEL
Godly leaders govern with divine counsel. Israel was made up of twelve tribes, each of which had a unique prophetic destiny. All together these twelve tribes constituted the government of God for Israel. With everyone functioning in their prophetic destinies, Israel was positioned to prosper spiritually, sociologically, and economically. "Without counsel, plans go awry, but in the multitude of counselors they are established" Proverbs 15:22. King David was known to harness the potentials of each tribe to build a very prosperous kingdom. He was able to take over all the territory assigned to Israel as a promise from God and laid

the foundation for a prosperous reign for his son Solomon. The sixth eye is to harness the potentials of strategic people God places in your life to govern your inheritance in Christ.

SEVENTH EYE – SPIRIT OF MIGHT

Godly leaders operate specifically within the scope of their authority. As human beings we all have several abilities and opportunities that come our way. However, our abilities may not be deployed for just any opportunity that comes our way. Though generally we have the power to do almost anything we set our minds to, to be effective and prosperous leaders, we must focus our abilities and resources to tackle opportunities within the framework of our divine assignment. The seventh eye is to deploy our potentials and authority within the jurisdiction of our inheritance in Christ Jesus.

Predators and Preys

In the book of Isaiah chapter eleven the scripture says: "The wolf also shall dwell with the lamb, the leopard shall lie down with the young goat, the calf and the young lion and the fatling together; and a little child shall lead them. The cow and the bear shall graze; their young ones shall lie down together; and the lion shall eat straw like the ox. The nursing child shall play by the cobra's hole, and the weaned child shall put his hand in the viper's den. They shall not hurt nor destroy in all My holy mountain, for the earth shall be full of the knowledge of the LORD as the waters cover the sea." Animals generally depict the character of man. People who display traits of the wolf, leopard, lion, bear and cobra are generally known as predators who will not miss an opportunity to devour their prey. A lamb within the reach of a wolf is equal to dinner. The only way predators and prey will dwell together in peaceful co-existence is an environment where godly leadership governs with revelation knowledge and prudence. When we all begin to identify, harness, and deploy our divine potentials within the framework of godly leadership, the earth will become a great place for everyone to prosper.

Leadership begins with the seven spirits. Jesus accomplished His mission on earth – not by decisions made by relying solely on the sight of his natural eyes or hearing of his ears. Jesus analyzed issues primarily from the spiritual perspective. A typical scenario is recorded in John 8:1-11, "Now early in the morning He came again into the temple, and all the people came to Him; and He sat down and taught them. Then the scribes and Pharisees brought to Him a woman caught in adultery. And when they had set her in the midst, they said to Him, "Teacher, this woman was caught in adultery, in the very act. Now Moses, in the law, commanded us that such should be stoned. But what do You say?" This they said, testing Him, that they might have something of which to accuse Him. But Jesus stooped down and wrote on the ground with His finger, as though He did not hear. So when they continued asking Him, He raised Himself up and said to them, "He who is without sin among you, let him throw a stone at her first." And again He stooped down and wrote on the ground. Then those who heard it, being convicted by their conscience, went out one by one, beginning with the oldest even to the last. And Jesus was left alone, and the woman standing in the midst. When Jesus had raised Himself up and saw no one but the woman, He said to her, "Woman, where are those accusers of yours? Has no one condemned you?" She said, "No one, Lord." And Jesus said to her, "Neither do I condemn you; go and sin no more." When the Jews brought the woman caught in adultery to Jesus, they had already judged her with the penalty of death for her sin. Secondly, they had resorted to a double standard by not bringing to Jesus the man who had also engaged with this woman in the act of adultery. Thirdly, they had observed that since Jesus constantly operated in a dimension of goodness and mercy, this would be a perfect trap to test his allegiance to the Law of Moses. Despite the factual evidence of having seen the woman in the act of adultery, it was obvious that they were operating with a double standard of concealed sins in their own lives. When Jesus put them to the test of mercy, their disappearance was clear evidence of their hypocrisy and wickedness.

Broken, Crushed and Pressed

There were three almond shaped knobs on each branch of the seven branched lamp stand. The oil from the two trees beside the lamp stand first flowed into the first knob, filled it before overflowing into the next knob. To extract oil from olives, they must first be broken to take out the seeds, then the seeds will be crushed to paste and then pressed to release the oil. Brokenness is the first stage in the process of building an anointed godly leader. Spiritually, brokenness signifies repentance. When we are convicted by God's word and make resolutions to turn away from sin, it is evidence of brokenness which is the first process in releasing our anointing. To be crushed is significant of a contrite spirit. When we take a step further after repentance to fast from all those pleasures that allure to sin and unrighteousness, we become contrite in spirit. There are certain sins that may not go away though we repent repeatedly. When we find ourselves trapped by such failings despite our repentance, it becomes necessary to go to the next level, which is to fast about it and trust for deliverance by the power of the blood of Jesus. Finally, the anointing that breaks the yoke is always deployed when we are pressed. Travailing prayer pressurizes our spirit to release the anointing. Everyone who wants to function in the dimension of godly leadership must travail until the oil starts to flow and their seven-branched lamp stand is ignited so they can walk in the perfect light of supernatural vision.

CHAPTER TWELVE

THE DUMB FACTOR

The Table of Showbread is where we feast with God. When Moses encountered God in the burning bush, Moses spoke with God and engaged Him in a conversation. Until you engage God in a conversation you are spiritually dumb. The most important person that you should ever speak to is God. Our opportunity to speak the words of God comes only when we feast with Him at the Table of Showbread. This is when God empowers us to speak His own words. Without feasting with God, the tendency is that we mostly say things that are outside the scope of our authority. We speak careless words. In Proverbs 9:1-6 scripture says: "Wisdom has built her house, She has hewn out her seven pillars; She has slaughtered her meat, She has mixed her wine, She has also furnished her table. She has sent out her maidens, She cries out from the highest places of the city, "Whoever is simple, let him turn in here!" As for him who lacks understanding, she says to him, "Come, eat of my bread and drink of the wine I have mixed. Forsake foolishness and live, And go in the way of understanding"

God set a feast and invited Moses to come and eat. God said I have seen the affliction of the children of Israel, and I have given you Moses the mandate to set them free. Moses said whom should I say has sent me when they ask. God said 'I Am' is My name. God gives us our mandate at the table where he feasts with us. Your mandate is the framework of your authority here on earth. Authority means delegated power, what you can do and cannot do. Your function and mission are all in your mandate. It is only when you sit down and feast with God that you receive your mandate from God. Prior to this time, Moses had never spoken with God before so even after the encounter he felt incapable of speaking. "Then Moses said to the LORD, "O my Lord, I am not eloquent, neither before nor since You have spoken to Your servant; but I am slow of speech and slow of tongue." So the LORD said to him, "Who has made man's mouth? Or who makes the mute, the deaf, the seeing, or the blind? Have not I, the LORD? Now therefore, go, and I will be with your mouth and teach you what you shall say." But he said, "O my Lord, please send by the hand of whomever else You may send." So the anger of the LORD was kindled against Moses, and He said: "Is not Aaron the Levite your brother? I know that he can speak well. And look, he is also coming out to meet you. When he sees you, he will be glad in his heart. Now you shall speak to him and put the words in his mouth. And I will be with your mouth and with his mouth, and I will teach you what you shall do. So he shall be your spokesman to the people. And he himself shall be as a mouth for you, and you shall be to him as God" Exodus 4:10-16. God rebuked Moses for complaining of not being eloquent. In the face of his creator, it was obviously a silly excuse. Moses was being sly, just like most people who may not want to go in the direction of divine destiny. He just did not want to confront the Pharaoh. God had given him eloquence, the ability to communicate and articulate his mindset with clarity.

Speaking about the end times, Jesus gave instruction to His disciples, "Then He said to them, "Nation will rise against nation, and kingdom against kingdom. And there will be great earthquakes in various places, and famines and pestilences; and there will be fearful sights and great signs from heaven. But before all these things, they will lay their hands on you and persecute you, delivering you up to the synagogues and prisons. You will be brought before kings and rulers for My name's sake. But it will turn out for you as an occasion for testimony. Therefore settle it in your hearts not to meditate beforehand on what you will answer;

for I will give you a mouth and wisdom which all your adversaries will not be able to contradict or resist" Luke 21:10-15. Stephen a follower of Jesus operated in this dimension, "And Stephen, full of faith and power, did great wonders and signs among the people. Then there arose some from what is called the Synagogue of the Freedmen (Cyrenians, Alexandrians, and those from Cilicia and Asia), disputing with Stephen. And they were not able to resist the wisdom and the Spirit by which he spoke" Acts 6:8-10. When Stephen was brought in trial before the council of the Jews, he spoke so eloquently under the inspiration of the Holy Spirit that the glory of God manifested, "When they heard these things they were cut to the heart, and they gnashed at him with their teeth. But he, being full of the Holy Spirit, gazed into heaven and saw the glory of God, and Jesus standing at the right hand of God, and said, "Look! I see the heavens opened and the Son of Man standing at the right hand of God!" Acts 7:54-56.

The Table of Showbread

Twelve loaves of bread, each to represent the tribes was laid on this table every week. When you feast with God at his table, you are delivered from spiritual dumbness. The dumb factor is evident when people do not take you seriously and are not convicted by what you say. This is an indication that you have no mandate, no authority and your words are not significant. When you speak words of authority, people listen and want to connect with you. They can hear your authority - they can hear the voice of God through you.

Royalty

The Table of Showbread had a molding like unto a crown at the top part of it. This was the place of royalty where kings feasted with God. When you constantly feast with the King of Kings, your words will always reflect your mandate. God gives you a voice that reflects your scope of authority. It was the place where Jesus sat down with his twelve disciples and broke bread and wine. There were twelve loaves of bread on the Table of Showbread. Each loaf represented an Israelite tribe. In the Holy Place you could not see the Table of Showbread which had on it the twelve loaves of bread without the seven branched lampstand. Each tribe had a loaf of bread assigned to them which was relevant of their provision from God. It was their mandate from God to prosper. The bread spoke to the earth, territory and wealth that was assigned to each tribe. The DNA of your wealth is in the bread. The bread is your empowerment to prosper in the place that God has assigned to you. "And you shall remember the Lord your God, for it is He who gives you power to get wealth, that He may establish His covenant which He swore to your fathers, as it is this day" Deuteronomy 8:18. Our covenant relationship with God is how we leverage wealth here on earth. When we worship at Church, receive the sermon and feast at the communion table is how we key into our authority. Think of yourself as a king in the presence of your overall source of authority. It is an opportunity to ask the questions on your mind. God answers our questions by giving us revelation during the delivery of His word. This is the time to understand how to tackle difficult issues within our various domains. All the other kings present also receive different understanding based on what they may have asked him about their sphere of authority. The bread reveals the scope of our authority as kings. The Apostle Paul puts it this way, "For this reason I bow my knees to the Father of our Lord Jesus Christ, from whom the whole family in heaven and earth is named, that He would grant you, according to the riches of His glory, to be strengthened with might through His Spirit in the inner man, that Christ may dwell in your hearts through faith; that you, being rooted and grounded in love, may be able to comprehend with all the saints what *is* the width and length and depth and height— to know the love of Christ which passes knowledge; that you may be filled with all the fullness of God. Now to Him who is able to do exceedingly abundantly above all that we ask or think, according to the power that works in us, to Him *be* glory in the church by Christ Jesus to all generations, forever and ever. Amen" Ephesians 3:15-21. First, when Paul talks about the height, breadth, width, and length of God's love for us, he is speaking of the scope of our authority. Whenever you buy a parcel of land, the indenture will define the dimensions of the property. It is the same with our assigned domain as believers in Christ. There are specific dimensions to our scope of authority which comes to us by divine revelation when we feast with the King of Kings. Secondly, Paul uses the word 'filled' to mean – we have eaten food and are satisfied so we have energy or power at work in us. Therefore, all that we can accomplish is through God, based on that reservoir of energy we have received from feasting with Him. We can do exceedingly, abundantly above all that we can or imagine according to His power at work in us.

Government

God gave Moses the mandate through dialogue. God said you are not going to leave Egypt empty handed. This was a mandate. Bring the people out but not poor. A mandate is a powerful thing. It means every knee shall bow as far as your destiny is concerned. That is the reason every tribe was represented by a precious stone. The foundation of the heavenly Jerusalem was decked with twelve precious stones representing the twelve apostles of Jesus. "Now the wall of the city had twelve foundations, and on them were the names of the twelve apostles of the Lamb. And he who talked with me had a gold reed to measure the city, its gates, and its wall. The city is laid out as a square; its length is as great as its breadth. And he measured the city with the reed: twelve thousand furlongs. Its length, breadth, and height are equal. Then he measured its wall: one hundred and forty-four cubits, according to the measure of a man, that is, of an angel. The construction of its wall was of jasper; and the city was pure gold, like clear glass. The foundations of the wall of the city were adorned with all kinds of precious stones: the first foundation was jasper, the second sapphire, the third chalcedony, the fourth emerald, the fifth sardonyx, the sixth sardius, the seventh chrysolite, the eighth beryl, the ninth topaz, the tenth chrysoprase, the eleventh jacinth, and the twelfth amethyst. The twelve gates were twelve pearls: each individual gate was of one pearl. And the street of the city was pure gold, like transparent glass" Revelations 21:14-21. You will notice that there were specific dimensions to God's holy city. God the Father is primarily the architect of all human life and inheritances. He gives dimension and scope which clearly defines everyone's inheritance in Christ. When we feast with Him at the Table of Showbread, we are able understand the full scope of our authority and jurisdictions. Though there are twelve loaves on the table, we only feast on one loaf. However, others to whom it belongs will take up the other eleven. The good thing here is that these other believers are a part of our government. No single tribe had what it took to benefit absolutely from the fullness of Christ if they did not function within the framework of government. It takes twelve to form a godly model of government that resonates with the heavenly design. Whatever your assignment here on earth, there are eleven uniquely gifted people that God brings your way to help constitute your government which you may refer to as Board of Directors, Management Team, or Committee.

Seed And Harvest In A Concurrent Era

Many people pursue careers that are lucrative and may build an impressive resume in an industry that may not reflect their prophetic destiny. Like Jesus, you seek to discover your government prayerfully. God will reveal these people through whom He will equip you to succeed. These people will constitute the Board of Directors of the organization that God has inspired you to set up.

Seed And Harvest In A Concurrent Era

CHAPTER THIRTEEN

THE DEAF FACTOR

This is the inability to hear the sounds of heaven and the voice of God, which can be a great impediment to our prosperity. When Jesus taught his disciples to pray, he revealed an important essence of synergy – "Thy kingdom come, Thy will be done on earth as it is in heaven" Matthew 6:9-13. Currently on this earth, there is no obvious indication that God's kingdom is being manifested. We see wickedness everywhere. The world at large operates as a lynch mob and the media often publishes information that incenses the vices in people.

God has a will that has to be manifested here on earth and yet they are not being manifested here on earth? We humans constantly reject the will of God otherwise, most people will attend church wanting to know God's will. When you answer to God's will, you become a channel to release his blessing. Most of the things we all need to become gratified in life are mostly within our reach but then, we are unable to have them because of disconnection with God's will. As a result, most people suffer in life and become bitter with the whole concept of a heavenly father responsible for our lives. The essence of being a conduit for the manifestation of God's will is our greatest challenge.

Moses was in exile tending the flock of his father-in-law. It was the lowest point of his life and yet he was a prince from Egypt. One day while leading the flock to find pasture, he got to the backside of the desert, which was the mountain of God. He saw a burning bush that was not consumed by the fire and turned aside to see the supernatural sight. God is constantly doing things to catch our attention, but we often do not turn aside to observe. When Moses turned aside to observe, he heard 'Moses, Moses'. For the first time he heard the voice of God his maker. The voice of God that you hear is how your deafness is healed. If you can hear the voice of God, you are no longer deaf. If you cannot hear the voice of God, you are deaf. You should desire to hear the clear voice of God. That is how the deaf factor is taken out of the way. Moses was no longer deaf because he could hear the voice of God.

Worship

The Altar of Incense was the part of the temple where worship took place. Our worship atmosphere is how we connect to heaven. When we come to God's presence, we experience the fullness of joy and liberty. Worship is all about answering to the activity going on in heaven. There must be a synergy between heaven and earth. This is only possible if we can hear heaven. We connect to hearing by our ears. We cannot do what is taking place in heaven if we are deaf. God needs partners, he needs people who love his will and desire the kingdom.

At the well in Samaria, Jesus asked the Samaritan woman for water, and she was surprised. The Samaritan woman said to him, "You are a Jew and I am a Samaritan woman. How can you ask me for a drink?" (For Jews do not associate with Samaritans.) Jesus answered her, "If you knew the gift of God and who it is that asks you for a drink, you would have asked him and he would have given you living water." "Sir," the woman said, "you have nothing to draw with and the well is deep. Where can you get this living water? Are you greater than our father Jacob, who gave us the well and drank from it himself, as did also his sons and his livestock?" Jesus answered, "Everyone who drinks this water will be thirsty again, but whoever drinks the water I give them will never thirst. Indeed, the water I give them will become in them a spring of water welling up to eternal life." The woman said to him, "Sir, give me this water so that I won't get thirsty and have to keep coming here to draw water." He told her, "Go, call your husband and come back." "I have no husband," she replied. Jesus said to her, "You are right when you say you have no husband. The fact is, you have had five husbands, and the man you now have is not your husband. What you have just said is quite true." "Sir," the woman said, "I can see that you are a prophet. Our ancestors worshiped on this mountain, but you Jews claim that the place where we must worship is in Jerusalem." "Woman," Jesus replied, "believe me, a time is coming when you will worship the Father neither on this mountain nor in Jerusalem. You Samaritans worship what you do not know; we worship what we do know, for salvation is from the Jews. Yet a time is coming and has now come when the true worshipers will worship the Father in the Spirit and in truth, for they are the kind of worshipers the Father seeks. God is spirit, and his worshipers must worship in the Spirit and in truth" John 4:9-24. Worship means 'worthy-ship', making God worthy. The favor of God manifests because somebody is willing to worship God. When you become God's channel for meeting the need in someone's life, they now have evidence of God's provision. People are not to belittle themselves for their needs so do not wait for people to beg you for their needs. Nothing we do on earth is of value if it does not reveal the worth of God.

Worship is a dimension of relationship that unveils royalty. Kings do not beg for what they need. Not long after David was anointed by the twelve tribes to the throne of Israel, king Hiram offered to build him a palace. "Now Hiram king of Tyre sent envoys to David, along with cedar logs and carpenters and stonemasons, and they built a palace for David. Then David knew that the LORD had established him as king over Israel and had exalted his kingdom for the sake of his people Israel" 2 Samuel 5:11&12. King Hiram came to minister to David's anointing. That is the essence of kingdom relationships. Those who recognize your domain will worship.

The Altar of Incense

Most people think of worship as just singing spiritual songs to adore God. Though it is one aspect of worship, singing alone is not total worship. The Altar of Incense which was significant of worship in the tabernacle of Moses was where special incense was offered. God gave them the recipe for incense that was to be offered up at the Altar of Incense. Four in all, they were frankincense, onycha, stacte and galbanum.

1. FRANKINCENSE

This significant of righteousness. When scriptures inspire us, we must confess them to invoke the righteousness of God into manifestation. This is how we get angels into action. Angels are energized to manifest the will of God when we declare those scriptures that strongly convict us. Most people who practice occult understand the power of spoken words much more than the average Christian. You will often see them chant words repeatedly while counting beads on the train or some other public place. They understand that if you can say these words to a certain degree, you will have your declarations manifested. God told Joshua "This Book of the Law shall not depart from your mouth, but you shall meditate in it day and night, that you may observe to do according to all that is written in it. For then you will make your way prosperous, and then you will have good success" Joshua 1:8. Though the word 'meditate' in the scriptures means to 'mutter' repeatedly, most Christians relate to it as though to think upon God's word. Thinking on God's word is one aspect of meditation but then as frankincense, it must be proclaimed to invoke the righteousness of God. There are many ways we find ourselves unable to function in the righteousness of God. For instance, there are many Christians who are addicted to fornication, pornography, lying, debauchery, wrath, malice, nicotine and many lusts of the flesh, which they have been unable to overcome in spite of praying, fasting and seeking deliverance. In such instances, invoking the righteousness of God by the declaration of God's word invokes angelic ministry. Remember that in the face of an earth without form, void and darkness, God proclaimed His word and they became a reality. This is how God intended Joshua to operate to become prosperous and have good success. We invoke the righteousness of God by declaring God's word to manifest in our lives. Whenever you are listening to God's word and some scriptures convict you strongly, you must deploy them by muttering it out for angels to carry out. Such actions of angels reveal the majesty of God and glorify Him. Once, as I was teaching on this aspect of worship at Church, the Holy Spirit impressed into my spirit 'if you do this, your dreams will come true'.

2. ONYCHA

This means to roar like a lion and prevail over our enemies, which is significant of praying in the spirit. "In the same way, the Spirit helps us in our weakness. We do not know what we ought to pray for, but the Spirit himself intercedes for us through wordless groans. And he who searches our hearts knows the mind of the Spirit, because the Spirit intercedes for God's people in accordance with the will of God" Romans 8:26, 27. When we pray in the Spirit, we avail ourselves for the Holy Spirit to intercede through us. Onycha is to make the voice of the blood of our redemption heard in the spiritual realm. Every time those in the occult chant words into the spirit realm, they set in motion demonic activity that robs us of what is due to us as children of God. Through the chanting and incantation of those who practice occult, curses are invoked upon believers because of trespasses. Demons that perpetuate curses against us back off because "There is therefore now no condemnation for those of us who dwell in Christ Jesus who walk not after the flesh but according to the Spirit". Romans 8:1. Curses are neutralized by the voice of the blood that Jesus shed for us on the cross at Calvary. When we travail in the Spirit, we smear that blood on what pertains to us in the spiritual and orchestrate divine protection. Remember the destruction angel did not kill the firstborn of the Israelite families who marked their doorposts with the blood of the Passover lamb.

3. STACTE

This to celebrate God's goodness using songs of adoration. "My heart is overflowing with a good theme; I recite my composition concerning the King; My tongue *is* the pen of a ready writer. You are fairer than the sons of men; Grace is poured upon Your lips; Therefore God has blessed You forever" Psalm 45:2. Stacte means to ooze by inspiration, to glorify God by inspiration. Often we sense a familiar song resound in our hearts. It is the choir of heaven ministering to you what activity is taking place in heaven on your behalf. It reflects what angels have been deployed over your life. You must do whatever it takes to get that music going. Many instances in scriptures reveal that whenever God is praised his enemies are destroyed. When a song comes into your heart, it is a manifestation of 'stacte', and in response you must rise to the occasion to sing it over and over. Join the angels and let the worship flow, celebrate the goodness of God and your enemies will be put to shame. Do not miss that moment. Connect, sing, dance and synergize with heaven.

4. GALBANUM

This to worship God with fat, which is significant of tithes and offerings. "Bring all the tithes into the storehouse, That there may be food in My house, And try Me now in this," Says the LORD of hosts, "If I will not open for you the windows of heaven And pour out for you such blessing That there will not be room enough to receive it" Malachi 3:10. Our tithes and offerings are the fat without which our worship is incomplete. In Deuteronomy 26, God instructed the Israelites to make pronouncements over their tithes. "When you have finished laying aside all the tithe of your increase in the third year—the year of tithing—and have given it to the Levite, the stranger, the fatherless, and the widow, so that they may eat within your gates and be filled, then you shall say before the LORD your God: 'I have removed the holy tithe from my house, and also have given them to the Levite, the stranger, the fatherless, and the widow, according to all Your commandments which You have commanded me; I have not transgressed Your commandments, nor have I forgotten them. I have not eaten any of it when in mourning, nor have I removed any of it for an unclean use, nor given any of it for the dead. I have obeyed the voice of the LORD my God, and have done according to all that You have commanded me. Look down from Your holy habitation, from heaven, and bless Your people Israel and the land which You have given us, just as You swore to our fathers, "a land flowing with milk and honey." You need to declare and instruct provision angels to release divine providence when you give your tithes in Church. The declaration means - I have done my part and so now God must do his part. When you are dumb, you make the angels deaf so they cannot hear you and honor your orders. Your pronouncements after tithing, triggers the synergy that must take place between the earth and heaven for the goodness of God to manifest.

Spontaneous Worship

Worship requires being always spontaneous. You must answer to divine inspiration. Staying connected with your angels, the sounds of heaven and the will of God. The glory of God will always manifest when you know how to connect with the works of God. At every point in time, you must be a willing worshipper. Worship is getting your angels to always work for you and with you. Though it may not be church service time, we have opportunity to always worship God, to synergize with angels and manifest God's kingdom here on earth. "But when He again brings the firstborn into the world, He says: "Let all the angels of God worship Him." And of the angels He says: "Who makes His angels spirits And His ministers a flame of fire" Hebrews 1:6&7. You must think of worship in the sense of the two reasons an airplane flies high in the skies. First is aerodynamics, which is how the exterior design of an aircraft makes it gain altitude quickly in resonance with the wind. The angels are the winds and our ability to synergize with angels is our aerodynamics. Second is the engine, which burns fuel to work the propellers to build thrust. When we worship in spirit and in truth, we spark fire in the spirit realm. We energize the works of God and set heaven in motion to favor our cause. There is a wind that will carry you to the highest heights. That wind is the manifestation of angels who carry out God's will. He makes his angels winds, and his servants flames of fire. Like a boat on water, worship is to deploy the sails of God in the presence of aiding winds. When you are not worshipping the winds are against you. However, when you worship, it puts the winds behind you to push you forward to your destiny.

Seed And Harvest In A Concurrent Era

CHAPTER FOURTEEN

THE DOUBT FACTOR

When God spoke to Moses about the assignment of delivering the Israelites out of Egypt, Moses was pessimistic about the possibility. "Then Moses answered and said, "But suppose they will not believe me or listen to my voice; suppose they say, 'The LORD has not appeared to you.' The issue of doubt was a fundamental obstacle that Moses envisaged will plague his attempt to deliver the Israelites out of Egypt. Moses needed the means to confront the reality of doubt as an impediment. "So the LORD said to him, "What is that in your hand?" He said, "A rod." And He said, "Cast it on the ground." So he cast it on the ground, and it became a serpent; and Moses fled from it. Then the LORD said to Moses, "Reach out your hand and take it by the tail" (and he reached out his hand and caught it, and it became a rod in his hand), "that they may believe that the LORD God of their fathers, the God of Abraham, the God of Isaac, and the God of Jacob, has appeared to you." Furthermore the LORD said to him, "Now put your hand in your bosom." And he put his hand in his bosom, and when he took it out, behold, his hand was leprous, like snow. And He said, "Put your hand in your bosom again." So he put his hand in his bosom again, and drew it out of his bosom, and behold, it was restored like his other flesh. "Then it will be, if they do not believe you, nor heed the message of the first sign, that they may believe the message of the latter sign. And it shall be, if they do not believe even these two signs, or listen to your voice, that you shall take water from the river and pour it on the dry land. The water which you take from the river will become blood on the dry land" Exodus 4:1-9. The rod turned into a snake, the leprous hands of Moses restored and the water turned into blood were three ways Moses was empowered to overcome the potential doubt in the mind of the Israelites. A rod is a ruler's insignia of authority, symbol of status, education, and role in society. Moses was a prince of Egypt, which is why he held that rod. God let him see what he had been so proud of all this while. As it were in the spirit, you are a venomous serpent. Your own rod based on the devil's authority is a serpent you will run from. God said pick it back up from an opposite direction. Previously you held the head but now you are going to hold the tail. It became a rod again. Before then, it was the rod of Moses, which was all that the world had made him to become. Nevertheless, for God to use him, he had to take what the world had taught him and turn it upside down. After picking the snake up from the tail it became a rod again, but this time it was called the 'Rod of God'.

One of the primary ways the devil prevents us from walking in victory and dominion is through the world's educational system. In addition, the acceptable standards of what goals we must achieve in society in order to be respected. The more you achieve educationally, the worldly accomplishments you attain and the higher you climb up the ladder of worldly status, the more you will be respected in society. Moses was a prince in that system until the system failed him. He inwardly cried to God until God gave him a mission. But then, he reasons that this mission is impossible in the face of doubt. Though it was God Almighty talking to him, he wanted to know how to deal with the issue of doubt.

Doubt takes place in the mind. The Apostle Paul understands this perfectly "For though we walk in the flesh, we do not war according to the flesh. For the weapons of our warfare are not carnal but mighty in God for pulling down strongholds, casting down arguments and every high thing that exalts itself against the knowledge of God, bringing every thought into captivity to the obedience of

Christ, and being ready to punish all disobedience when your obedience is fulfilled" 2 Corinthians 10:3-6. Paul says the greatest strongholds are not in the material things we have but rather in the state of our mind. The most significant stronghold we must overcome is the state of our minds. The mind is the place of doubt, mindsets, and thoughts contrary to the will of God. Doubt is any thought contrary to the will of God. Paul says though we live in the reality of a material world, we do not necessarily become victorious by possessing material things rather it is the state of our minds. In Philippians 3:3-21, the Apostle Paul chronicles how this understanding has influenced his appreciation of walking with Christ. "For we are the circumcision, who worship God in the Spirit, rejoice in Christ Jesus, and have no confidence in the flesh, though I also might have confidence in the flesh. If anyone else thinks he may have confidence in the flesh, I more so: circumcised the eighth day, of the stock of Israel, of the tribe of Benjamin, a Hebrew of the Hebrews; concerning the law, a Pharisee; concerning zeal, persecuting the church; concerning the righteousness which is in the law, blameless. But what things were gain to me, these I have counted loss for Christ. Yet indeed I also count all things loss for the excellence of the knowledge of Christ Jesus my Lord, for whom I have suffered the loss of all things, and count them as rubbish, that I may gain Christ and be found in Him, not having my own righteousness, which is from the law, but that which is through faith in Christ, the righteousness which is from God by faith; that I may know Him and the power of His resurrection, and the fellowship of His sufferings, being conformed to His death, if, by any means, I may attain to the resurrection from the dead. Not that I have already attained, or am already perfected; but I press on, that I may lay hold of that for which Christ Jesus has also laid hold of me. Brethren, I do not count myself to have apprehended; but one thing I do, forgetting those things which are behind and reaching forward to those things which are ahead, I press toward the goal for the prize of the upward call of God in Christ Jesus." The Apostle Paul willingly relinquished all his credentials as an outstanding lawyer, Pharisee, and status of Roman citizenship in the face of the revelation of Christ. His impact afterwards as an Apostle of Christ was clearly phenomenal, outstanding, and everlasting.

An Old Testament scenario where the Philistines were in confrontation with Israel reveals the potency of this reality of victory through mindset. "And a champion went out from the camp of the Philistines, named Goliath, from Gath, whose height was six cubits and a span. He had a bronze helmet on his head, and he was armed with a coat of mail, and the weight of the coat was five thousand shekels of bronze. And he had bronze armor on his legs and a bronze javelin between his shoulders. Now the staff of his spear was like a weaver's beam, and his iron spearhead weighed six hundred shekels; and a shield-bearer went before him. Then he stood and cried out to the armies of Israel, and said to them, "Why have you come out to line up for battle? Am I not a Philistine, and you the servants of Saul? Choose a man for yourselves, and let him come down to me. If he is able to fight with me and kill me, then we will be your servants. But if I prevail against him and kill him, then you shall be our servants and serve us." And the Philistine said, "I defy the armies of Israel this day; give me a man, that we may fight together." When Saul and all Israel heard these words of the Philistine, they were dismayed and greatly afraid" 1 Samuel 17:4-11. When David came up against Goliath he was not concerned with the significantly sophisticated armory of Goliath. On the contrary, all the Israelites were intimidated by the sophistication of the armory of Goliath. David declared openly that the Lord does not save by sword or spear. He saw beyond the armory. He said to Goliath, you have defied the armies of the living God. David sized him up spiritually, 'you uncircumcised Philistine'. He measured him up in the light of God's standards of righteousness. This is a major factor that will be responsible for your victory over any kind of opposition. How do you see God? And how do you see your opposition? Though King Saul provided David with a physical armor to challenge Goliath, he was not comfortable with it. David began to recount his achievements in the wilderness. He had killed a lion and a bear that came after the sheep he was taking care of. David declared that the same God who had delivered him from the attack of the lion and bear would give him victory over Goliath. Victory is always accomplished first in the mind. We must articulate what God has done in our lives in the face of our enemies and circumstances.

Moses' summary of the potential opposition to his mission was one word 'doubt'. God said; "what do you have in your hands?" Moses responds, my status, I am a prince of Egypt. God said 'okay let's put it in perspective. You are still carrying a rod that indicates you are a prince of Egypt, but then you are in exile. Now that you can see the spiritual reality of what you are proud of, you are running away from it. That is exactly why though you still holding the rod as a prince of Egypt you are afraid to confront the Pharaoh. You cannot come against a system with the very authority you received from them. Therefore, God says – 'if you will pick the life and education Egypt gave you, approach it from the opposite direction, you will begin to operate in signs, wonders and miracles. Egypt trained you and you were moving in that direction, but you murdered and you are now in exile. Now you can go back as my Prince, and deliverer my people by wielding divine authority and approaching the mission from divine perspective.

The Veil

Within the framework of the Tabernacle of Moses, the veil is the object of opposition to our mission. The veil is the place of doubt. That was where the serpent tricked Eve. He played with her mind. 'Did God really say...' he got Eve to doubt God. Every purpose to your life attracts doubt and fear. The moment you doubt God, fear enters your soul. By the spirit of fear, the devil attempts to intimidate, defeat, and conquer us. The Tabernacle of Moses was structured with objects of worship that facilitate us with the Spirit of Sonship by which we overcome any element of fear and demonic intimidation. "For as many as are led by the Spirit of God, these are sons of God. For you did not receive the spirit of bondage again to fear, but you received the Spirit of adoption by whom we cry out, "Abba, Father." The Spirit Himself bears witness with our spirit that we are children of God" Romans 8:14-16. As children of God, we are clothed with the spiritual robes that qualify us to enter God's Most Holy Place to experience the manifestation of His glory. The veil was made up of five colors – Fine linen, Scarlet, Gold, Purple and Blue.

1. FINE LINEN

Fine Linen speaks of the righteousness of God. It is manifested when we confess scriptures that allure to the righteousness of God to challenge the works of the devil to that standard. There is an interesting story in 2 Chronicles 13 that is testimony to the righteousness of God invoked in warfare against the unrighteous. "And there was war between Abijah and Jeroboam. Abijah set the battle in order with an army of valiant warriors, four hundred thousand choice men. Jeroboam also drew up in battle formation against him with eight hundred thousand choice men, mighty men of valor. Then Abijah stood on Mount Zemaraim, which is in the mountains of Ephraim, and said, "Hear me, Jeroboam and all Israel: Should you not know that the LORD God of Israel gave the dominion over Israel to David forever, to him and his sons, by a covenant of salt? Yet Jeroboam the son of Nebat, the servant of Solomon the son of David, rose up and rebelled against his lord. Then worthless rogues gathered to him, and strengthened themselves against Rehoboam the son of Solomon, when Rehoboam was young and inexperienced and could not withstand them. And now you think to withstand the kingdom of the LORD, which is in the hand of the sons of David; and you are a great multitude, and with you are the gold calves which Jeroboam made for you as gods. Have you not cast out the priests of the LORD, the sons of Aaron, and the Levites, and made for yourselves priests, like the peoples of other lands, so that whoever comes to consecrate himself with a young bull and seven rams may be a priest of things that are not gods? But as for us, the LORD is our God, and we have not forsaken Him; and the priests who minister to the LORD are the sons of Aaron, and the Levites attend to their duties. And they burn to the LORD every morning and every evening burnt sacrifices and sweet incense; they also set the showbread in order on the pure gold table, and the lampstand of gold with its lamps to burn every evening; for we keep the command of the LORD our God, but you have forsaken Him. Now look, God Himself is with us as our head, and His priests with sounding trumpets to sound the alarm against you. O children of Israel, do not fight against the LORD God of your fathers, for you shall not prosper!" But Jeroboam caused an ambush to go around behind them; so they were in front of Judah, and the ambush was behind them. And when Judah looked around, to their surprise the battle line was at both front and rear; and they cried out to the LORD, and the priests sounded the trumpets. Then the men of Judah gave a shout; and as the men of Judah shouted, it happened that God struck Jeroboam and all Israel before Abijah and Judah. And the children of Israel fled before Judah, and God delivered them into their hand. Then Abijah and his people struck them with a great slaughter; so five hundred thousand choice men of Israel fell slain. Thus the children of Israel were subdued at that time; and the children of Judah prevailed, because they relied on the LORD God of their fathers. And Abijah pursued Jeroboam and took cities from him: Bethel with its villages, Jeshanah with its villages, and Ephrain with its villages. So Jeroboam did not recover strength again in the days of Abijah; and the LORD struck him, and he died." In this scenario God fought against Jeroboam because King Abijah invoked the righteousness of God as a standard. Whenever we proclaim God's righteousness as a standard of judgment against our adversaries, God fights for us, and the curtain called Fine Linen makes way for us to experience the glory of God.

2. SCARLET

Scarlet speaks of redemption. The two common names of our spiritual adversary 'Devil' and 'Satan' reveals how he operates to block our access to the throne room of God. Devil is the compound of 'do evil'. He bombards our minds with ideas to 'do evil' and when we succumb to his temptation, he turns around to his function as Satan, meaning 'the accuser'. He goes before God to accuse us for our sins. "Then I heard a loud voice saying in heaven, "Now salvation, and strength, and the kingdom of our God, and the power of His Christ have come, for the accuser of our brethren, who accused them before our God day and night, has been cast down. And they overcame him by the blood of the Lamb and by the word of their testimony, and they did not love their lives to the death" Revelations 12:10&11. In addition to the word of our testimony, we overcame the accuser by the blood of Jesus Christ which was shed on the cross of Calvary. The blood of Jesus gives us access through the red color of the veil. In the face of adversity and attacks from the kingdom of darkness, we must invoke the testimonies of God. Whenever the enemy comes against us, no matter his form or size, we must rehearse what God has done in the past. The book of Judges chapter six recounts how Gideon was selected to lead Israel to confront the Midianites who were oppressing them. He was constantly recounting the testimonial of how God had delivered their forefathers out of the Egyptian slavery so an angel was sent to him. "Now the Angel of the LORD came and sat under the terebinth tree which was in Ophrah, which belonged to Joash the Abiezrite, while his son Gideon threshed wheat in the winepress, in order to hide it from the Midianites. And the Angel of the LORD appeared to him, and said to him, "The LORD is with you, you mighty man of valor!" Gideon said to Him, "O my lord, if the LORD is with us, why then has all this happened to us? And where are all His miracles which our fathers told us about, saying, 'Did not the LORD bring us up from Egypt?' But now the LORD has forsaken us and delivered us into the hands of the Midianites." Then the LORD turned to him and said, "Go in this might of yours, and you shall save Israel from the hand of the Midianites. Have I not sent you?" So he said to Him, "O my Lord, how can I save Israel? Indeed my clan is the weakest in Manasseh, and I am the least in my father's house." And the LORD said to him, "Surely I will be with you, and you shall defeat the Midianites as one man." Then he said to Him, "If now I have found favor in Your sight, then show me a sign that it is You who talk with me. Do not depart from here, I pray, until I come to You and bring out my offering and set it before You." And He said, "I will wait until you come back." So Gideon went in and prepared a young goat, and unleavened bread from an ephah of flour. The meat he put in a basket, and he put the broth in a pot; and he brought them out to Him under the terebinth tree and presented them. The Angel of God said to him, "Take the meat and the unleavened bread and lay them on this rock, and pour out the broth." And he did so. Then the Angel of the LORD put out the end of the staff that was in His hand, and touched the meat and the unleavened bread; and fire rose out of the rock and consumed the meat and the unleavened bread. And the Angel of the LORD departed out of his sight. Now Gideon perceived that He was the Angel of the LORD. So Gideon said, "Alas, O Lord GOD! For I have seen the Angel of the LORD face to face." Then the LORD said to him, "Peace be with you; do not fear, you shall not die." So Gideon built an altar there to the LORD, and called it The-LORD-Is-Peace. To this day it is still in Ophrah of the Abiezrites. Now it came to pass the same night that the LORD said to him, "Take your father's young bull, the second bull of seven years old, and tear down the altar of Baal that your father has, and cut down the wooden image that is beside it; and build an altar to the LORD your God on top of this rock in the proper arrangement, and take the second bull and offer a burnt sacrifice with the wood of the image which you shall cut down." So Gideon took ten men from among his servants and did as the LORD had said to him. However, because he feared his father's household and the men of the city too much to do it by day, he did it by night. First of all, Gideon was chosen as an instrument to orchestrate Israel's deliverance because he was recounting the testimonies of God's deliverance of Israel. That had been his constant heartbeat and prayer. The angel told him to gather courage and walk in the fullness of his authority as a child of God. Secondly, God told him to destroy the altar of Baal in his father's house. The blood sacrifice that was offered from that altar was a hindrance to God's deliverance. Once Gideon mustered the courage to believe in the God who had delivered Israel in the past and destroyed the altar of Baal, offering sacrifices to God instead, he was used as an instrument of deliverance. It was quite an easy victory where with only three hundred people blowing horns and breaking empty pitchers, they defeated the Midianites. Redemption comes by declaring God's testimonies and invoking the blood of Jesus.

3. GOLD

Gold is significant of divinity. "As His divine power has given to us all things that pertain to life and godliness, through the knowledge of Him who called us by glory and virtue, by which have been given to us exceedingly great and precious promises, that through these you may be partakers of the divine nature, having escaped the corruption that is in the world through lust" 2 Peter 2:3&4. When we embrace the promises of God for our lives, it inspires us to avoid lustfulness. Once we begin to pray for knowledge of God's plan for our lives, it's as though we have made a request for God to equip us with His nature that overcomes the lust to sin. We automatically invoke the divine nature, which is the work of the Holy Spirit that facilitates us to walk in the Spirit. The world gave Moses and Paul ambition until Moses encountered God in a burning bush while Paul encountered Jesus Christ on the road to Damascus. God gave Moses a supernatural vision that redirected the course of his life, empowered him to operate supernatural signs, wonders and miracles. Similarly, Paul was given a divine assignment that was characterized with manifestations of supernatural signs, wonders and miracles. Signs, wonders and miracles are divine interruptions of nature on behalf of God's children. You cannot pursue God's plan for your life by walking in the flesh. "But also for this very reason, giving all diligence, add to your faith virtue, to virtue knowledge, to knowledge self-control, to self-control perseverance, to perseverance godliness, to godliness brotherly kindness, and to brotherly kindness love. For if these things are yours and abound, you will be neither barren nor unfruitful in the knowledge of our Lord Jesus Christ. For he who lacks these things is shortsighted, even to blindness, and has forgotten that he was cleansed from his old sins. Therefore, brethren, be even more diligent to make your call and election sure, for if you do these things you will never stumble; for so an entrance will be supplied to you abundantly into the everlasting kingdom of our Lord and Savior Jesus Christ" 2 Peter 1:5-11. The pursuit of ambition is the key motivation to operate the lust of the flesh, lust of the eyes and pride of life.

When the Apostle Paul was in pursuit of ambition, he was used by Satan to work havoc against the Church. He persecuted the Christians from city to city until he encountered Christ. All along, he thought he was doing

Seed And Harvest In A Concurrent Era

God a favor by persecuting the Church. Without the knowledge of God's plan, most religious people ignorantly frustrate God's work. Without a supernatural vision of God's plan, we pursue ambition and become victims of the lusts of the flesh. "I say then: Walk in the Spirit, and you shall not fulfill the lust of the flesh. For the flesh lusts against the Spirit, and the Spirit against the flesh; and these are contrary to one another, so that you do not do the things that you wish. But if you are led by the Spirit, you are not under the law. Now the works of the flesh are evident, which are: adultery, fornication, uncleanness, lewdness, idolatry, sorcery, hatred, contentions, jealousies, outbursts of wrath, selfish ambitions, dissensions, heresies, envy, murders, drunkenness, revelries, and the like; of which I tell you beforehand, just as I also told you in time past, that those who practice such things will not inherit the kingdom of God. But the fruit of the Spirit is love, joy, peace, longsuffering, kindness, goodness, faithfulness, gentleness, self-control. Against such there is no law. And those who are Christ's have crucified the flesh with its passions and desires. If we live in the Spirit, let us also walk in the Spirit. Let us not become conceited, provoking one another, envying one another" Galatians 5:16-26. There is a constant internal war that takes place within every believer. The spirit and flesh of the believer are constantly at variance with each another. Our spirit is aware of God's plan and how we keep track with the promises of God. Our flesh on the other hand has an insatiable appetite for those things that bring immediate gratification and pleasure. As it were, both spirit and flesh seek to bring us some form of satisfaction hence the battle within.

While the goal of the spirit is to align us with God's eternal plan that ushers us into destiny, the goal of the flesh is to align with Satan's mission to steal, kill and destroy us. Our soul is the middle ground where the battle takes place. It is our soul that ultimately determines whether we yield to the dictates of our spirit or the lust of the flesh. To lure us toward hell and destruction, the Devil triggers these lusts that appeal so strongly to our soul - adultery, fornication, uncleanness, lewdness, idolatry, sorcery, hatred, contentions, jealousies, outbursts of wrath, selfish ambitions, dissensions, heresies, envy, murders, drunkenness, revelries. Simultaneously the Holy Spirit intervenes to influence us towards divine destiny by prompting the fruit of the Spirit - love, joy, peace, longsuffering, kindness, goodness, faithfulness, gentleness, self-control. With our soul we can process these offers and decide who to yield ourselves to. If we are inclined towards immediate gratification of our aspirations and desires, we end up yielding to the lust of the flesh. However, if we are heavenly minded and aspire to press towards destiny then we reject the lust of the flesh and yield to the fruit of the Holy Spirit. When we walk in the fruit of the spirit, the golden door opens and gives us access to the throne room of God.

4. PURPLE

Purple is the color significant of royalty. Kings exercise their mandate to fight for and defend their territories. Everyone on earth is assigned some space as a divine inheritance for which they must fight and protect. Back in the Garden of Eden, God gave Adam the mandate to 'dress it and keep it'. The devil came and lured Adam and Even into sin and disfavor with God. This way, Adam lost the mandate of reigning in the Garden of Eden and was exiled to live in hardship outside the Garden. The restoration process starts with accepting where God has carved out as our inheritance. There is a place or sphere of life that represents the territory where God expects us to reign as kings. If our ancestors or parents already secured it and passed on the legacy to us, our mandate will be to protect it. However, if we did not inherit a legacy, then we have the mandate to fight for our space or domain as well as protect it from aggressors. When King David was anointed king over all the tribes of Israel, he went to war with all the nations who occupied the land that God had promised to Israel. "After this it came to pass that David attacked the Philistines and subdued them. And David took Metheg Ammah from the hand of the Philistines. Then he defeated Moab. Forcing them down to the ground, he measured them off with a line. With two lines he measured off those to be put to death, and with one full line those to be kept alive. So the Moabites became David's servants, and brought tribute. David also defeated Hadadezer the son of Rehob, king of Zobah, as he went to recover his territory at the River Euphrates" 2 Samuel 8:1-3. We must engage the kingdom of darkness in warfare for every territory that belongs to us by the allocation of God Almighty. The purple curtain answers only to those who intend to access the throne room of God as true representatives of their domains. If you come toward the veil bearing a flag other than your space, access to the throne room will be denied.

5. BLUE

Blue is the color significant of Sonship. Obedience to the Holy Spirit is the essence of Sonship. "For as many as are led by the Spirit of God, these are sons of God. For you did not receive the spirit of bondage again to fear, but you received the Spirit of adoption by whom we cry out, "Abba, Father." The Spirit Himself bears witness with our spirit that we are children of God, and if children, then heirs—heirs of God and joint heirs with Christ, if indeed we suffer with Him, that we may also be glorified together" Romans 8:14-17. The unique quality that distinguishes sons from hirelings is the virtue of endurance when things do not work out well in an estate. The hireling will immediately look for an alternative job or revenue source. Once their wages cannot be guaranteed they will immediately abandon the estate. However, sons will remain on the estate and endure through hardships and difficult times until there is a change. The kingdom of darkness sometimes launches attacks to orchestrate hard times for believers. In such times, the key to victory is perseverance. If we suffer with him we shall also be glorified with him. "Though He was a Son, yet He learned obedience by the things which He suffered. And having been perfected, He became the author of eternal salvation to all who obey Him" Romans 5:8-9. Suffering adversity and enduring through it was how Jesus learned obedience. We must obey even when victory is not immediately eminent. The blue curtain opens to those who have overcome persecution and adversity through perseverance.

All the devil does to prevent us from experiencing the goodness of God is to trigger doubt in our minds. Stop focusing on those physical things that seem to be the obstacles and start your war against doubt, fear and the carnal mind and ultimately every veil or obstacle to the manifestation of the glory of God will begin to give way.

CHAPTER FIFTEEN

THE GUILT FACTOR

In the most holy place of the tabernacle of Moses was placed the last object of fellowship with God, known as the 'Ark of the Covenant'. There were three aspects to the Ark of the Covenant – The Cherubim, The box containing the stone engraving of the Ten Commandments and the Mercy Seat. Firstly, the cherubim are angelic beings significant of the 'rhema'. This is divine revelation that comes to us as angelic visitations, prophecies, visions, and dreams. Secondly, the stone engraved with the written word of God is what is known in Greek as 'Logos'. It is the entirety of the scriptures. Thirdly, the mercy seat is where God unveils His judgment. "And the cherubim shall stretch out their wings above, covering the mercy seat with their

255

wings, and they shall face one another; the faces of the cherubim shall be toward the mercy seat. You shall put the mercy seat on top of the ark, and in the ark you shall put the Testimony that I will give you. And there I will meet with you, and I will speak with you from above the mercy seat, from between the two cherubim which are on the ark of the Testimony, about everything which I will give you in commandment to the children of Israel" Exodus 25:20-22. The Ark of the Covenant was the place of judgment. The High Priest went to the most holy place once a year to receive the judgments of God that were revealed at the Ark of the Covenant. Once in a year, God judges His people based on how they have conducted themselves previously and in the light of His future agenda.

The Cherubim, The Ten Commandments and the Mercy Seat are the three aspects of the Ark of the Covenant that are significant of the primary factors that influence God's judgments. First of all, God judges us based on the extent to which we obeyed the 'Logos' which is the written word of God found in the scriptures. Secondly, God judges us based on how well we obeyed the 'Rhema' or divine revelation that comes through angelic visitation, prophesies, visions and dreams. Thirdly, God judges us based on how merciful we have been. "If you really fulfill the royal law according to the Scripture, "You shall love your neighbor as yourself," you do well; but if you show partiality, you commit sin, and are convicted by the law as transgressors.

Seed And Harvest In A Concurrent Era

For whoever shall keep the whole law, and yet stumble in one point, he is guilty of all. For He who said, "Do not commit adultery," also said, "Do not murder." Now if you do not commit adultery, but you do murder, you have become a transgressor of the law. So speak and so do as those who will be judged by the law of liberty. For judgment is without mercy to the one who has shown no mercy. Mercy triumphs over judgment" James 2:8-13.

We all will most likely be guilty of not fully obeying the 'Logos' and 'Rhema'. However, Mercy is where we can make up for our shortcomings. How we dispensed mercy to others is the ultimate determinant of God's judgment. "Blessed are the merciful, for they shall obtain mercy" Matthew 5:7. We must score very well in how we dispensed mercy to others in order to experience God's judgment of promotion and elevation. Mercy is primarily based on initiative. Jesus tells the story of the Good Samaritan as a demonstration of mercy. "And behold, a certain lawyer stood up and tested Him, saying, "Teacher, what shall I do to inherit eternal life?" He said to him, "What is written in the law? What is your reading of it?" So he answered and said, "'You shall love the LORD your God with all your heart, with all your soul, with all your strength, and with all your mind,' and 'your neighbor as yourself.'" And He said to him, "You have answered rightly; do this and you will live." But he, wanting to justify himself, said to Jesus, "And who is my neighbor?" Then Jesus answered and said: "A certain man went down from Jerusalem to Jericho, and fell among thieves, who stripped him of his clothing, wounded him, and departed, leaving him half dead. Now by chance a certain priest came down that road. And when he saw him, he passed by on the other side. Likewise a Levite, when he arrived at the place, came and looked, and passed by on the other side. But a certain Samaritan, as he journeyed, came where he was. And when he saw him, he had compassion. So he went to him and bandaged his wounds, pouring on oil and wine; and he set him on his own animal, brought him to an inn, and took care of him. On the next day, when he departed, he took out two denarii, gave them to the innkeeper, and said to him, 'Take care of him; and whatever more you spend, when I come again, I will repay you.' So which of these three do you think was neighbor to him who fell among the thieves?" And he said, "He who showed mercy on him." Then Jesus said to him, "Go and do likewise." Luke 10:30-37. The Good Samaritan was justified because he had mercy and compassion on his neighbor. Mercy is unleashed by initiative, prerogative and choice. You encounter a situation where someone needs help and you do not turn a blind eye to it. Though our obedience to the Logos and Rhema are equally important factors that determine God's judgment, mercy is the most important of them all. Mercy gives everyone whether they are believers or unbelievers the privilege to experience the good judgment of God. This means that in situations where others are in need of help, we also have the opportunity to dispense judgment. We make the decision to be of help or to look the other way.

To execute the mandate of delivering the Israelites out of Egypt, God sent Moses as a 'god' to judge Pharaoh. God put his will in the heart of Moses. "Is not Aaron the Levite your brother? I know that he can speak well. And look, he is also coming out to meet you. When he sees you, he will be glad in his heart. Now you shall speak to him and put the words in his mouth. And I will be with your mouth and with his mouth, and I will teach you what you shall do. So he shall be your spokesman to the people. And he himself shall be as a mouth for you, and you shall be to him as God. And you shall take this rod in your hand, with which you shall do the signs" Exodus 4:14-17. God gave Aaron to be Moses' spokesperson, while Moses was to function as a 'god' to the Pharaoh. Our hearts are the temple of the living God, and we are His agents of divine judgment. He puts judgment in us because we are gods made in His image and likeness. Though in a court of law everyone usually argues with a sound case based on the law and evidence available, the judge passes judgment based on prerogative. We all pass judgment every day in our work in relation to co-workers, clients and customers as well as in society in relation to family, friends and people we meet on the streets. Every one of us constantly passes judgment every day but then every year God passes judgment on how we passed judgment.

For four hundred years the Egyptians had the opportunity to judge Israel however they wished. In the light of God's covenant with Abraham several years earlier, it was time to pass judgment on the Egyptians and so Moses was bearing the Ark of the Covenant in his heart to do exactly so. Speaking from the Ark of the Covenant in his heart, Moses declares God's judgment to the Pharaoh 'let my firstborn Israel go and serve me, If not I will kill your firstborn'. After four hundred years of slavery, it was judgment time. Pharaoh was the head of Egypt, which was symbolic of the kingdom of darkness. Pharaoh stands in the place of Satan. Israel had served the Egyptians and received nothing for their work. Now it was time to restore what was owed to them and set them free. God instructed Moses to take the rod to manifest God's signs, wonders and miracles. When Moses went to confront the Pharaoh, the Pharaoh objected: "I do not know the God you are talking about so why should I let Israel go..." Moses judged the Pharaoh in ten ways that God expects every human being to dispense mercy.

1. WATER IS TURNED INTO BLOOD

We drink water to quench our thirst. "On the last day, that great day of the feast, Jesus stood and cried out, saying, "If anyone thirsts, let him come to Me and drink. He who believes in Me, as the Scripture has said, out of his heart will flow rivers of living water." But this He spoke concerning the Spirit, whom those believing in Him would receive; for the Holy Spirit was not yet given, because Jesus was not yet glorified" John 7-37-39. Water is significant of inspiration. How have you inspired others? The world inspires people in a way that kills them, a way of blood. Most movies we watch center around crime, the lyrics of worldly songs are negative, violent video games for kids is how the seed of violence is sown in them. God passed a guilty verdict on both the Egyptians and Israelites when their water turned into blood. God has given us the potential to inspire people either with blood or water. The world inspires people to death. As believers we inspire one another to life. God judges us every year based on how we have inspired our world. Inspiration is always based on initiative. It is based on prerogative. If you come to my house on a visit, I can decide to show you a very violent movie or a godly movie. When you leave my house, what seed would I have sown into you. The children of Israel were all guilty as well. That judgment was both upon the Israelites and Egyptians for seven days.

2. THE PLAGUE OF FROGS

Moses struck the water of the Nile with his rod and frogs came out of it scattering themselves all over Egypt. Frogs live comfortable on land as well as in water. Frogs represent sexual perversion and immorality. These acts are represented by the frog spirit. This judgment was everywhere. Both the Israelites and Egyptians were guilty. Jesus said immorality takes place in the mind and not necessarily when the act takes place. The second plague was judgment against every act of immorality.

3. THE PLAGUE OF LIES

Lice are insects that pollinate. Butterflies are positive insects because they take pollen from one plant to another to facilitate fruitfulness. We also have insects like mosquitoes that sting people, take a virus from their blood and deposit it another person's body. Therefore, we have positive and negative insects. We are either pollinating good or evil by the examples we set for others in society. Whenever you observe people around you and notice them exhibiting positive qualities you do not have, you may adopt those fine qualities and exhibit them in your environment. Someone else will notice you exhibiting these qualities and learn from you. Those who observe you may change their lives as a result. Your life can either be a blessing or otherwise. There are people you never want to be like because these people pollinate evil. It does not take a big mosquito to kill you. Every time we demonstrate goodness, we are pollinating the works of God and consequently changing lives by this impact. People will endure through their challenges because you also did so or give up because you set the wrong standard. The Egyptians as well as the Israelites were all guilty so they all experienced the plague of lice.

4. THE PLAGUE OF FLIES

Flies are informants. They spread both wrong and right information. Mostly however, those who spread any information they have not confirmed as fact, end up fueling gossip. Gossip is the root of character assassination. We are sometimes victimized over a long period when false information is passed around and people speak evil of our character. Most often, in order to sell great volumes of publication some media houses spread lies by twisting the facts. We are judged by the information we spread. The Israelites were judged innocent. God made a distinction between the Israelites and the Egyptians in the fourth plague. Only the Egyptians suffered this plague because they alone were guilty.

5. THE PLAGUE OF CATTLE DISEASE

Moses invoked judgment on all the cattle of the Egyptians. Cattle speak of character. We either possess a godly character or an ungodly character. When we display godly character, we refrain from wickedness or hurting others in society. Ungodly character makes us act as vicious predators in character – undermining and destructive. The plague of cattle disease was a judgment on the character of the Egyptians. The Israelites were deemed innocent.

6. THE PLAGUE OF BOILS

Moses invoked the plague of boils, which broke out on the bodies of every Egyptian. Infirmity in the body is often related directly or indirectly to what we eat. The boils came because of what they ate. Not everything edible is good for your body. Your body is the temple of God and so you cannot eat just everything. God told the children of Israel what food they could eat and not eat. The Patriarchs ate the food that God told them was good for their body and so they lived long. You are judging your body when you eat food not good for your body. God can have a great purpose for your life, but you can judge your body and die prematurely. Fasting is how we abstain from eating unclean food.

7. THE PLAGUE OF HAIL

Hail and fire rained down from heaven on Egypt. Snow and rain are good, and they come from heaven but when hailstones and fire come down from heaven, it is an indication of judgment on the atmosphere. "For My thoughts *are* not your thoughts, Nor *are* your ways My ways," says the LORD. "For *as* the heavens are higher than the earth, So are My ways higher than your ways, And My thoughts than your thoughts. "For as the rain comes down, and the snow from heaven, And do not return there, But water the earth, And make it bring forth and bud, That it may give seed to the sower and bread to the eater, So shall My word be that goes forth from My mouth; It shall not return to Me void, But it shall accomplish what I please, And it shall prosper *in the thing* for which I sent it" Isaiah 55:8-11. Thoughts results into ways. What you think, hope, desire is what you request from God. God is constantly looking at our desires. Your desire is like your whole world, which is your space in the realm of the spirit. Therefore, in the realm of the spirit, God sees your desires. What is your desire? Is it that people should be saved or condemned? Do you desire apostasy or revival? Some people fight the worship of God in their communities and some Christians even oppose revival. There are people who cannot desire good for anybody. What is your request for your society? When your desire is not for good it invokes hail and fire that comes down. The Egyptians were guilty of evil desires, so they experienced the judgment of hail, which destroyed everything they had on the fields.

8. THE PLAGUE OF LOCUST

The locust came and ate up the vegetation. There were three trees in the Garden of Eden that God allowed man to cultivate. The tree pleasant of the sight is significant of our emotional, marital or family destiny. The tree good for food is significant of our profession, career, or financial destiny. The tree of life is significant of our priestly or spiritual destiny. Plants speak of our three-fold destiny which we discover by seeking God. You cannot just pursue anything that makes sense to you on this earth. You must find God's purpose for your life and fulfill it. Are you walking in God's purpose for your life? The Egyptians were guilty of not pursuing divine destiny, so their vegetation was destroyed by the plague of locust.

9. THE PLAGUE OF DARKNESS

At the prompting of Moses, the sun did not give light for three days so there was darkness all over Egypt. "But we have renounced the hidden things of shame, not walking in craftiness nor handling the word of God deceitfully, but by manifestation of the truth commending ourselves to every man's conscience in the sight of God. But even if our gospel is veiled, it is veiled to those who are perishing, whose minds the god of this age has blinded, who do not believe, lest the light of the gospel of the glory of Christ, who is the image of God, should shine on them. For we do not preach ourselves, but Christ Jesus the Lord, and ourselves your bondservants for Jesus' sake. For it is the God who commanded light to shine out of darkness, who has shone in our hearts to give the light of the knowledge of the glory of God in the face of Jesus Christ" 2 Corinthians 4:2-6. There are three components of darkness - dishonesty, craftiness, and deceitfulness. The truth is God's perspective of any given situation. The revelation of truth is how we experience the light of God. Jesus said "I am the way the truth and the light". God has called us to be the light of this world and when we walk in that light, darkness will not have power over us. The Egyptians were guilty of operating in dishonesty, craftiness, and deception so they experienced the judgment of darkness that manifested for three days.

10. THE DEATH OF THE FIRSTBORNS

God entered covenant with the children of Israel before he killed the first born of the Egyptians. The covenant of tithing requires believers to give the first tenth of their income to their local Church. The covenant of tithing is our acknowledgement of God as our source of provision and protection. Those who do not tithe are guilty of not acknowledging God as their source of providence and preservation. When you tithe, God judges those holding your stuff and judges you for restoration. The Egyptians were guilty, so their firstborns died in one night by the action of the destruction angel. Pharaoh eventually gave the order for Israel to get out Egypt with a restoration of their wealth.

Overall, the Israelites scored seven out of ten so the glory of God showed up to lead them out of Egypt to inherit the Promised Land. Every year when we are judged in all these ten areas our score determines our elevation in life.

Seed And Harvest In A Concurrent Era

Part IV

Seed And Harvest In A Concurrent Era

CHAPTER SIXTEEN

'CONCURRENT ERA' STANDARDS

To understand what fully happens in our world in this concurrent era, scriptures provide prophetic insight. "The word of the LORD came again to me, saying: "Son of man, when a land sins against Me by persistent unfaithfulness, I will stretch out My hand against it; I will cut off its supply of bread, send famine on it, and cut off man and beast from it. Even if these three men, Noah, Daniel, and Job, were in it, they would deliver only themselves by their righteousness," says the Lord GOD.

Seed And Harvest In A Concurrent Era

"If I cause wild beasts to pass through the land, and they empty it, and make it so desolate that no man may pass through because of the beasts, even though these three men were in it, as I live," says the Lord GOD, "they would deliver neither sons nor daughters; only they would be delivered, and the land would be desolate.

"Or if I bring a sword on that land, and say, 'Sword, go through the land,' and I cut off man and beast from it, even though these three men were in it, as I live," says the Lord GOD, "they would deliver neither sons nor daughters, but only they themselves would be delivered.

"Or if I send a pestilence into that land and pour out My fury on it in blood, and cut off from it man and beast, even though Noah, Daniel, and Job were in it, as I live," says the Lord GOD, "they would deliver neither son nor daughter; they would deliver only themselves by their righteousness."

For thus says the Lord GOD: "How much more it shall be when I send My four severe judgments on Jerusalem—the sword and famine and wild beasts and pestilence—to cut off man and beast from it? Yet behold, there shall be left in it a remnant who will be brought out, both sons and daughters; surely they will come out to you, and you will see their ways and their doings. Then you will be comforted concerning the disaster that I have brought upon Jerusalem, all that I have brought upon it. And they will comfort you, when you see their ways and their doings; and you shall know that I have done nothing without cause that I have done in it," says the Lord GOD" Ezekiel 14:12-23.

This prophecy gives insight into four ways God judges the earth as well as the three standards that survive the judgment. Famine, Beasts, Sword, and Pestilence are mentioned as four ways the world is judged. Obviously, these are the judgments directed towards the four walls of the worldly systems that encompass our emotional, spiritual, and financial fulfillment. Interestingly, the only survivors are Noah, Daniel, and Job. Let us first discuss the four kinds of judgment and then go on to the triple 'A' standards that survive the judgment.

a. Famine – Economic Hardship

Presently more than a third of the United States which is the largest grower of food in the world is going through drought conditions. Many states record rainfall patterns that are far lower than normal and some communities who were previously self-sufficient in water supply now import water to survive. Spiritually famine is significant of economic hardship, which currently plagues over seventy percent of the world's population. Most people today are living below the poverty line and struggle to meet their daily necessities of food, clothes, and shelter. Corporations who hire thousands of employees are constantly scaling down the size of their human resource and resorting to outsourcing and other ways of trimming down their liabilities. This trend will only resort in the increase of unemployment and the consequent rise of poverty. To compound this, there is a fight in the United States between Republicans and Democrats as to the level of entitlements paid out to the unemployed. Ultimately, the government will not be able to afford to meet the obligations of social security and other benefits for the unemployed. Without prognostication, we can clearly see that there is a famine that is way beyond our ability as humans to address. The famine is evidence of divine judgment already manifesting in the global economy and most people are suffering the effects in one way or the other. The declaration of austerity measures by governments will result in delays with payment of salaries and entitlements. Corporations will equally be justified to delay the wages of their human resource as well as payment to clients. It will not be uncommon for workers and contractors to wait for months at a time before receiving payment for services rendered.

b. Wild Beasts – Wickedness

In the jungle, wild beasts feed on vulnerable and defenseless prey. These wild beasts are significant of predators that perpetuate evil schemes against potential prey in society. The word predator should immediately ring the bell for some of us who are familiar with the practices of banks and financial institutions who lend money to individuals through consumer credit cards. These financial institutions have employed the services of lobbyists who fight for their interests in the government. No matter how much the government does to protect individuals from these predators, the lobbyists always rein in such influence in the design of legislation that ensures that the financial institutions always emerge winners. The prey will always remain prey in the face of these wild beasts. Corporations who provide basic utility services such as electricity, gas, telephone, and housing also operate like predators. Like financial institutions, they engage the services of lobbyists who fight for their interests so that individuals remain constant prey to their schemes. Most people must maintain two or more jobs just to keep up with bills from basic services. Parents cannot have enough time to spend with the families because it may come with the cost of eviction or denial of basic services. The rate of corporate greed and wickedness is so high and its effect on our sociological prosperity so alarming, we need no prognostication to realize that it is a judgment by itself on society. In the Concurrent Era, wicked people who are most often members of the occult will be open about their beliefs and practice evil publicly. Some will invoke demonic activity and incorporate witchcraft in their work as well as broadcast their rituals on the media for all to observe.

c. Sword – Crime

The level of crime in society today is so high that setting up penitentiaries has become a lucrative private venture in some nations. In the United States, there are private penitentiaries that are contracted by the governments to keep criminals convicted to prison sentences. Murder, rape and robberies are the top stories in any news cycle to the extent that crime sells better as a news item than community development stories. Most of the video games and movies by which we entertain ourselves must feature violent crimes to garner high patronage. Kids go to school with weapons and engage in mass massacre of teachers and fellow students. Increasingly, unsuspecting individuals go to public places and commit suicide bombings with the intention of killing as much people as they can. More people are procuring firearms now than at any other point in history. While some have noble intentions of using them for recreational hunting and self-defense, others procure these firearms with diabolical intentions. The escalation of firearms in the hands of so many in society is frightening and a trend that could turn peaceful demonstrations for instance into violent massacres. The increased crime rate is an obvious manifestation of judgment on society.

d. Pestilence – Climate Disruptions

While scientific research has facilitated most of the technological development responsible for our advancement as humans, high levels of industrial pollution and careless practices threaten the stability of our ecosystem. The Corporate world will do just about anything to increase profits. Though most manufacturing companies are often aware of the environmental consequences of their production processes, they ignore the effects of their activities. Unfortunately, they have politicians on their side who have blocked their conscience to this reality and so it is difficult to find enough support for legislation to curb practices that threaten the stability of the ecosystem. Failure to 'replenish the earth' which is one of the most important instructions to man, is why the weather patterns are changing so rapidly that we are at the brink of 'time collision' where the weather is hardly predictable, the ecological balance is lost, and we may become victims of the full consequence of global warming. Climate changes will result in new epidemics and an alarming rate at which diseases spread such that we may struggle to find immediate amelioration. Water and locally grown food is already in short supply in some communities as the environment is subjected to unfavorable and irregular weather patterns.

Assignment – Abstinence - Abundance

The 'time era', an age of 'might' where people prospered by leveraging philosophy, ambition, facts and sentiments to deploy resources ends with the year 2012. In the 'concurrent era' that follows, 'consecration', which is to be dedicated to God through sacrifice, will be the key to prosperity. Though most of the four judgments we have described from the prophecy of Ezekiel are already taking place to some extent, in the Concurrent Era, there will be a significant increase in those manifestations across the globe. These judgments will destroy the four walls of worldly system upon which governmental, business, institutional and professional endeavors thrived. To survive these four kinds of judgment we must embrace virtues epitomized by the lives of Noah, Daniel and Job. The credit rating agencies of the 'Time Era' will fail to provide credible assessment of organizations, institutions and individuals. Rather the virtues of Noah, Daniel and Job, which are the core elements of consecration, will become the new standards that qualify us for emotional, spiritual and financial prosperity.

I.   Noah – Assignment

In the Concurrent Era, the 'firstling' status is when you fulfill your divine assignment. Noah built an ark at the request of God. He was given specifications as to how to build it. God also gave Noah instructions concerning what animals to bring into the ark. When Noah had done what God instructed him, God closed the door of the ark and sent the flood. The flood preserved Noah, his family and all the animals with him in the ark. Everyone outside the ark was destroyed. During the concurrent era, fulfilling your divine assignment is the act of building an ark that will preserve you from the judgment that will be unveiled on the earth. Any member of your family that does not fulfill their divine assignment will not be automatically spared from the

Seed And Harvest In A Concurrent Era

judgment because of your status quo with God. Everyone will be personally accountable for how they invest their life, time, and resources. Whatever is your choice of profession, career, business investment or project endeavoring must be a mandate from God to garner divine favor. In the concurrent era, fulfilling your divine assignment is the seed that qualifies you for a harvest. Whether you operate as an individual or corporate entity, you will prosper by sowing seeds of purpose. The status of employed or unemployed will not be relevant in the concurrent era. Everyone will have to operate the mindset of 'self-employed', reaching out to those who need their impact. After sowing your seed of impact on others, you will not pressurize them to pay up, rather you will trust God for a harvest which will come in due season. Corporations that will survive and emerge very successful will be those who hire firstlings as their top executives. The Chief Executive Officer, Chief Operating Officer and Chief Financial Officer and as many as are in top management must be walking in divine purpose or else they will lead the enterprise into the ditch. Any government leadership that will make significant progress must assign firstlings to occupy top political positions. Heads of State Departments or Ministers of State should be assigned by divine purpose and not necessarily by academic or other standards.

II.   Daniel – Abstinence

During the concurrent era, what will qualify you for divine preservation is abstinence by revelation. When Daniel and his three Hebrew friends, Hananiah, Mishael and Azariah were selected for special indoctrination by King Nebuchadnezzar and assigned food dedicated to idols, they refused to contaminate themselves with it. They chose rather to feed on water and vegetables they picked from the fields. This way they avoided been contaminated with demonic food covenants so that God could fill them with divine wisdom. Their actions paid off and Daniel was promoted to Prime Minister of the world under the control of King Nebuchadnezzar. Because of his consecration, God gave Daniel an excellent spirit so he could understand all dreams and mysteries. When Daniel's enemies plotted against him and he was thrown into the lion's den, these wild animals did not harm him in any way. Just as Daniel was supernaturally preserved from the beasts, everyone who will learn abstinence by revelation will save themselves from the judgments of the concurrent era. Not every job, not every opportunity, not every method of investment, not every process of productivity, not every strategy for marketing, not every kind of friend, not every potential spouse, not every event, not every kind of food, not every drink may be good for you, if the voice of abstinence gives signals of restraint to your spirit. In the concurrent era, you ought to have an excellent spirit to be strategic. Your choice of concepts and methods for achieving goals must align with the wisdom of God. Whatever option you choose that defies divine counsel will fail to produce the expected results. Corporations that will excel must establish a Corporate Affairs Department headed by someone spiritually inclined. The role of the Corporate Affairs Officer will be to bring alignment of all corporate rules and practices in line with scriptural requirements. Government authorities will do well to revoke laws that are anti-scripture and reintroduce the Ten Commandments in schools and public places.

III.   Job – Abundance

In this era, the third way that qualifies you for divine favor is abundance of sacrifice. Job was known to be one of the richest in his day. He owned lots of cattle, sheep and camels significant of a huge enterprise. He had a wonderful family with seven sons and three daughters. In one day, he lost all his wealth and children. Worst of all he lost his health and became so deformed that his friends could not recognize him easily. All these calamities were because Satan had made a request to tempt Job. Satan's intention was to subject Job to so much pressure that he will reject the existence of a loving and good God. Job had to endure through poverty and pain for several days. Most of his friends did not empathize with him but rather accused him of pride and wrongdoing as diagnosis for his calamities. God was observing the character of Job in all that he had to suffer for maintaining a good testimony and trust in God's goodness. At the end of the trial, God restored a double of all that Job had lost. Whatever loss we endure unduly to evil schemes of the kingdom of darkness would be restored to us in good measure, pressed down, shaken together, and running over. Regardless of whether we are acknowledged or not, we must be willingly to sacrifice abundantly under the inspiration of the Holy Spirit.

The indicators by which you gauge how your investment prospers will change in this era so though your mind may not fully comprehend, do not hold back when prompted to do good and increase the level of your investments in any venture or project. Corporations that will prosper and take the lead in industry will be those who dedicate at least ten percent of their profits as tithes. For any government to thrive economically, they will have to develop effective welfare programs that cater for the poor.

ABOUT THE BOOK

Economic uncertainties, natural disasters, geopolitical conflicts, and crime are all on the steep rise across the globe. Is there any significance?

'Seed and Harvest In A Concurrent Era' explains the two periods our world has undergone – Pre-flood and Post-flood. pre-flood is the 'timeless' period between Adam and Noah while the post-flood is the 'time' era from Noah until now. The 'Time Era', an age of 'might' where people prospered by leveraging philosophy, ambition, facts, and sentiments to deploy resources has now ended.

We have been ushered into another phase where the 'Timeless' and 'Time' eras are running simultaneously. This is what is described in this book as the 'Concurrent Era'. Consecration, which is to commit ourselves to God through sacrifice, will be the way to prosperity. There will be major changes in the investment climate, enterprise and professional pursuit, weather patterns and much more.

In this book, I share my insights of how spiritual time unfolds in relation to our calling in Christ and the world system. You will learn how the primary objects of worship in the tabernacle enhances our spiritual senses to excel in a higher dimension.

ABOUT THE AUTHOR

Kenneth Walley is the Overseer of New Faith Tabernacle, a Charismatic/Pentecostal Church located at Fair Lawn, New Jersey. He is bi-vocational and serves as the President of Cibunet Corporation as well as KWI, a leadership development Institute. Endowed with an apostolic teaching ministry, he has authored several books including: 'Hexagon Quadrilateral' and 'American Culture in Water, Blood, Oil and Bread'. Ken has an unusual burden for revival and has conducted meetings across North America, Europe, and the continent of Africa with notable signs, deliverances, and healings.

www.ingramcontent.com/pod-product-compliance
Lightning Source LLC
Chambersburg PA
CBHW071944110426
42744CB00030B/285